# Sisters of the Yam
## Black Women and Self-Recovery

## by bell hooks

## South End Press          Boston, MA

DEC - - 1994

Printed in the United States.
Text design and layout by the South End Press collective
Cover design by Julie Ault and Gloria Watkins
Cover photo by Lorna Simpson, Waterbearer, 1986, used courtesy of Josh Baer Gallery, NYC.


**Library of Congress Cataloging-in-Publication Data**
Hooks, Bell.
Sisters of the yam : black women and self-recovery / by Bell Hooks.
    p.    cm.
    Includes bibliographical references.
    ISBN 0-89608-456-6 (pbk.) : $14.00. -- ISBN 0-89608-457-4 (cloth) : $30.00
1. Afro-American women--Mental health. 2. Self-esteem in women. 3. Self-actualization (Psychology). 4. Oppression (Psychology) I. Title.
RC451.5.N4H66    1993
155.8'496073--dc20                                              93-22112
                                                                   CIP


**South End Press, 116 Saint Botolph St., Boston, MA 02115**

99 98 97 96 95 94 93                    1 2 3 4 5 6 7 8 9

Celebrating the life and work
of Toni Cade Bambara
whose visionary insight, revolutionary spirit,
and passionate commitment to struggle
guides and sustains.

"Just so's you're sure, sweetheart,
and ready to be healed,
cause wholeness is no trifling matter.
A lot of weight when you are well."

—Toni Cade Bambara, *The Salt Eaters*

# Table of Contents

**Preface**

# Reflections of Light

When I wrote *Ain't I a Woman: Black Women and Feminism* twenty years ago, the chapter that most spoke to me was "Continued Devaluation of Black Womanhood." Concluding that chapter, I wrote:

> Widespread efforts to continue devaluation of black womanhood make it extremely difficult and often-times impossible for the black female to develop a positive self-concept. For we are daily bombarded by negative images. Indeed, one strong oppressive force has been this negative stereotype and our acceptance of it as a viable role model upon which we can pattern our lives.

Since I first wrote these words, the white-dominated mass media have changed little in the way in which they represent black women. We have changed. In the last twenty years black women have collectively challenged both the racism and sexism that not only shape how we are seen but determine how everyone interacts with us. We have resisted continued devaluation by countering the dominant stereotypes about us that prevail in white-supremacist capitalist patriarchy by decolonizing our minds. Here decolonization refers to breaking with the ways our reality is defined and shaped by the dominant culture and asserting our understanding of that reality, of our own experience.

In a revolutionary manner, black women have utilized mass media (writing, film, video, art, etc.) to offer radically different images of ourselves. These actions have been an intervention. We have also dared to move out of our "place" (that is away from the bottom of everything, the place this society often suggests we should reside). Moving ourselves from manipulatable objects to self-empowered subjects, black women have by necessity threatened the status quo. All the various groups—white men, white women, black men, etc.—that have imagined that black women exist to be the "mules of the world," providing service to others, have had to cope with our collective refusal to occupy this position. This challenge to the status quo has generated serious anti-black female backlash. The kind of backlash that combines fierce racism with anti-feminism, the kind that journalist Susan Faludi does not even begin to consider in her best selling book *Backlash: The Undeclared War Against Women*. Indeed, Faludi's work erases any focus on the way in which race is a factor determining degrees of backlash. That she could completely ignore the specificity of race, and once again construct women as a monolithic group whose common experiences are more important than our differences, heralds the acceptance of an erasure within the realms of popular feminist books—works written to reach mass audiences—of all the work black women and women of color have done (in conjunction with white allies in struggle) to demand recognition of the specificity of race.

Perhaps no other issue more glaringly showed that masses of white women still do not understand the interconnectedness of systems of domination, of racism and sexism, than the Clarence Thomas Supreme Court nomination hearings. Masses of white women rallied to Anita Hill's defense, all the while insisting that her race was not important and that the "real" issue was gender. Many of them simply would not break through denial and ignorance of the way white supremacy is instutionalized to see that had Anita Hill been a white woman accusing a black man of sexual harassment there would have been no television spectacle exposing her to the voyeuristic gaze of the masses. The forces of white-supremacist patriarchy would have demanded respect for her privacy, for her womanhood, a respect denied Anita Hill. The Thomas hearings served notice to black feminist thinkers and our allies in struggle that we must be ever vigilant in our efforts to resist devaluation, that it is a mistake for us to think that we have "arrived," that our political efforts to transform society and to be seen as subjects and not objects have been realized. That struggle continues.

The rise in black anti-feminism, often spearheaded by a focus on endangered black masculinity, has rekindled false assumptions that black women's efforts to resist sexism and sexist oppression are an attack on black life. To the contrary, renewed black liberation struggle can only be successful to the extent that it includes resistance to sexism. Yet there are masses of black people who are encouraged by sexist and misogynist black male and female leaders to believe that uppity black women are threatening our survival as a race. This backlash requires that those of us who are aware be ever vigilant in our efforts to educate one another, and all black people, for critical consciousness. Backlash, from whatever source, hurts. It retards and obstructs freedom struggle. Intense attacks help create a context of burnout and despair. It is crucial that black women and all our allies in struggle, especially progressive black men, seize the day and renew our commitment to black liberation and feminist struggle.

In my daily life practice as a teacher, writer, and activist, I work hard to find ways of sharing feminist thinking, black liberation struggle, with diverse groups of people, not just those of us who are involved in academic institutions. Years of inventing strategies to reach a broader audience have convinced me that we need to explore all outlets to share information. It was the success of the self-help book *Women Who Love Too Much* that convinced me that women of all races, classes, and sexual preferences would read work that addressed their concerns and most importantly their pain and their longing to transform their lives. This book, however, like many other self-help books for women, disturbed me because it denied that patriarchy is institutionalized. It made it seem that women could change everything in our lives by sheer acts of personal will. It did not even suggest that we would need to organize politically to change society in conjunction with our efforts to transform ourselves.

Mind you, since I have consistently used self-help literature to work on areas in my life where I have felt dysfunctional, I have tremendous respect for this literature whatever its limitations. For those among us who cannot afford therapy, or who have had endless hours of therapy that just did not work, it helps to have these other guides. For some time now, too, I have seen that we cannot fully create effective movements for social change if individuals struggling for that change are not also self-actualized or working towards that end. When wounded individuals come together in groups to make change our collective struggle is often undermined by all that has not been dealt with emotionally. Those of us committed to feminist movement, to black liberation struggle, need to work at self-actualization. In the anthology *The Black Woman,* Toni Cade Bambara reminded us that "revolution begins in the self and with the self." She urged us to see self-actualization as part of our political efforts to resist white supremacy and sexist oppression.

Many of us have longed to see the union of our political efforts to change society and our efforts to be individually self-actualized. We have wanted to politicize movements for self-recovery. Yet, working to help educate black females for critical consciousness, I often find that folks felt they did not have time for political work because they felt there were so many things messed up in their psyches, or in their daily lives, that they were just barely keeping a hold on life. Frankly, they are often more concerned with getting their lives together than with larger political issues, issues that did not seem to intersect with this need or promise to enhance this quest. This perspective is understandable, but much too limited. It ignores too much of the world around us. Desiring to create a context where we as black females could both work on our individual efforts for self-actualization and remain connected to a larger world of collective struggle led me to consider writing a self-help book that would especially address our concerns. I felt such a book would speak to black women and to everyone else that wanted to know us, and perhaps even themselves, better.

Meditating long and hard on Audre Lorde's essay "Eye to Eye" was the catalyst urging me to push harder to write work that would address a wider audience of black women. In her essay, Audre Lorde urges black females to put our struggle to self-actualize at the center of our daily life. She taught us,

> Learning to love ourselves as Black women goes beyond a simplistic insistence that "Black is beautiful." It goes beyond and deeper than the surface appreciation of Black beauty, although that is certainly a good beginning. But if the quest to reclaim ourselves and each other remains there, then we accept another superficial measurement of self, one superimposed upon the old one and almost as damaging, since it pauses at the superficial. Certainly it is no more empowering. And it is empowerment—our strengthening in the service of ourselves and each other, in the service of our work and future—that will be the result of this pursuit.

Living the teaching of Lorde inspired me to write this book on self-recovery, a book that would particularly address the needs and concerns of black women.

In the last twenty years, many black women have had the joy of ecstatic sustained bonding with one another. We have witnessed the power of sisterhood. We have experienced self-recovery. We have known, and continue to know, the rewards of struggling together to change society so that we can live in a world that affirms the dignity and presence of black womanhood. In many ways *Sisters of the Yam: Black Women and Self-Recovery* is a manifestation of that joy and an expression of the awareness that we must be ever vigilant—that the struggle continues.

## Introduction

# Healing Darkness

Sisters—and you who are our friends, loved ones, and comrades—I greet you in love and peace. This Saturday afternoon is a beautiful spring day, where the world is overflowing with beauty and splendor. Every aspect of nature is full of life. That which appeared dead but was merely dormant is beginning to grow again. Symbolized by holy days that celebrate resurrection and renewal, this is a time for all things to be made new—a joyous time. This morning as I went for walking meditation, I felt as though the world around me—the birds, the flowers, the newly cut green grass—was all a soothing balm, the kind Big Mama would spread on various parts of our body for any little old ailment. We thought her homemade salves had magical healing powers when we were children. Now, I am convinced that the magic, that power to heal, resided in her warm, loving, brown hands—hands that knew how to touch us and make us whole, how to make the hurt go away.

This is a book about healing, about ways to make the hurt go away. Like all the books I have written, it comes to me from places dark and deep within me, secret, mysterious places, where the ancestors dwell, along with countless spirits and angels. When I was a girl, Mama's father, Daddy Gus, taught me that everything in life was a dwelling place for spirits, that one only had to listen to hear their voices. The spiritual world of my growing up was thus very akin to those described in novels by Toni Morrison, Paule Marshall, or Ntosake Shange. There was in our daily life an ever present and deep engagement with the mystical dimensions of Christian faith. There was the secret lore of the ancestors—the Africans and Native Americans—who had given that new race of black folk, born here on this portion of earth, whole philosophies about how to be One with the universe and sustain life. That lore was shared by the oldest of the old, the secret believers, the ones who had kept the faith. There was the special magic of the Caribbean that was present in the form of Voudoun, that way of working roots my father's mother Sister Ray knew about (or so everyone said). And I remember most that people feared her—that she was seen as a woman of power.

Having lived in a segregated southern black world and in an integrated world, where black people live with and among whites, the difference I see is that in the traditional world of black folk experience, there was (and remains in some places and certainly in many hearts) a profound unshaken belief in the spiritual power of black people to transform our world and live with integrity and oneness despite oppressive social realities. In that world, black folks collectively believed in "higher powers," knew that forces stronger than the will and intellect of humankind shaped and determined our existence, the way we lived. And for that reason these black people learned and shared the secrets of healing. They knew how to live well and long despite adversity (the evils caused by racism, sexism, and class exploitation), pain, hardship, unrelenting poverty, and the ongoing reality of loss. They knew joy, that feeling that comes from using one's powers to the fullest. Despite the sexism of that segregated black world, the world of spirituality and magic was one where black women teachers, preachers, and healers worked with as much skill, power, and second sight as their black male comrades. Raised in such an environment, I was able to witness and learn. And yet, like the old ones before me who had been required by circumstance to willingly or unwillingly leave their ancestral home, I left that world of my beginning and entered the strange world of a predominantly white elitist university setting. I took with me to that world, however, ways of knowing and understanding reality I was determined to keep and hold. They were my links to life-affirming black cultural traditions. And indeed it was the will and way of the ancestors that sustained me during that time of my life, that sustains me still.

For the past twenty years I have been most concerned with learning book knowledge about many subjects. I decided to be a writer when I was still at home, still in grade school, and of course made public announcements and shared my work with family and friends. Everyone agreed that I had talent. I could act and I could write. I went away to college to study drama and everyone believed that I would one day come home, to the world of my ancestors, and be a teacher in the public schools. I did not return. In the years before she died, Baba, my Mama's mother, would often ask me "Glory, how can you live so far away from your people?" I knew what her words meant. She was asking how it was I could live without the daily communion and community of ancestors, kin, and family—how I could sustain my reason for living since I had been raised to believe that these connections gave life substance and meaning. I had no answer for her. I hung my head so that she could not see the tears in my eyes. I could not honestly say that I had found new community, new kin. I only knew that I was inhabited by a restless roaming spirit that was seeking to learn things in a world away from my people. Much of what I learned in that world was not life-affirming. Longing to become an intellectual, I stayed in college. I learned some important information. I became a strong and defiant critical thinker expressing my ideas publicly in the production of feminist theory, literary criticism, and more recently, cultural criticism. The artist inside me was most visible in private space. There I thought and dreamed about the world of my ancestors. I longed for the richness of my past, to hear again the wisdom of the elders, to sit at their feet and be touched by their presence.

Living and working in predominantly white settings, in situations where black people seem confused and uncertain about politics and identity, I began to think deeply about the way in which the collective lives of black people in contemporary white-supremacist patriarchy have become fundamentally estranged from life-affirming world views and life practices. Many black people see themselves solely as victims with no capacity to shape and determine their own destiny. Despite powerful anti-racist struggle in this society, expressed in the sixties' civil rights and black power movements, internalized racism manifested by ongoing self-hate and low self-esteem has intensified. Devastating poverty and the rising gaps between black folks who have gained access to economic privilege and the vast majority who will seemingly remain forever poor make it difficult for individuals to build and sustain community. Kinship ties between black people are more easily threatened and broken now than at other historical moments when even material well-being was harder for black people to gain than it is now. Widespread addiction, pervasive among all classes of black people, is yet another indication of our collective crisis. Black people are indeed wounded by forces of domination. Irrespective of our access to material privilege we are all wounded by white supremacy, racism, sexism, and a capitalist economic system that dooms us collectively to an underclass position. Such wounds do not manifest themselves only in material ways, they effect our psychological well-being. Black people are wounded in our hearts, minds, bodies, and spirits.

Though many of us recognize the depth of our pain and hurt, we do not usually collectively organize in an ongoing manner to find and share ways to heal ourselves. Our literature has helped, however. Progressive black women artists have shown ongoing concern about healing our wounds. Much of the celebrated fiction by black women writers is concerned with identifying our pain and imaginatively constructing maps for healing. Books like *Sassafrass, Cypress and Indigo; The Bluest Eye; The Color Purple; Praisesong for the Widow; Maru; The Salt Eaters;* and many others address the deep, often unnamed psychic wounding that takes place in the daily lives of black folks in this society. This fiction is popular because it speaks to the hurt black folks are grappling with. Indeed, many non-black people also find healing maps in this work they can use in daily life. It has been in my role as a professor, teaching the work of black writers in general, and black women writers in particular, that I became more fully aware of our contemporary collective suffering. Teaching young black people at one of the most prestigious universities in this society, I was amazed by their lack of self-awareness and understanding, their lack of knowledge of black history and culture, and the profound anxiety and despair that was so pervasive in their lives.

When black female students would come to my office after reading these novels and confess the truth of their lives—that they were terrorized psychologically by low self-esteem; that they were the victims of rape, incest, and domestic violence; that they lived in fear of being unmasked as the inferiors of their white peers; that stress was making their hair fall out; that every other month one of them was attempting suicide; that they were anorexic, bulimic, or drug addicted—I was shocked. Most of these students were coming from materially privileged backgrounds. Yet I saw in their lives the same problems that are so acutely visible among the black poor and underclass, problems that are usually seen by liberals in the larger society as rooted primarily in economics. What the experiences of these young black women indicated, however, was that the problem was not merely economic. This, of course, made sense to me. I had been raised in a world of the black poor and underclass that was still life-affirming. I knew that poverty by itself need not be a condition that promotes such nihilism and despair.

When black female students read Toni Bambara's novel *The Salt Eaters* in my black women writers course, several came to talk with me about their identification with the black woman character Velma, a character who attempts suicide when the novel opens. Hearing these women describe their sense of estrangement and loneliness, I felt that a support group was needed and helped organize it. There is this passage in *The Salt Eaters* where the black women ancestors, one living, one dead, come together to see about healing Velma. The younger of the two, Minnie Ransom, says to the elder: "What is wrong, Old Wife? What is happening to the daughters of the yam? Seem like they just don't know how to draw up the powers from the deep like before."

I strongly identified with this passage. Knowing that I had been raised among black women and men who were in touch with their healing powers, who had taught me how to "draw up the powers from the deep," I grieved for this new generation who seemed so modern, so sophisticated, and so lost. And I thought we should call our support group "Sisters of the Yam" to honor Bambara's work and the wisdom she offered to us. I also felt the "yam" was a life-sustaining symbol of black kinship and community. Everywhere black women live in the world, we eat yam. It is a symbol of our diasporic connections. Yams provide nourishment for the body as food yet they are also used medicinally—to heal the body.

Our collective hope for the group was that it would be a space where black women could name their pain and find ways of healing. The power of the group to transform one another's lives seemed to be determined by the intensity of each individual's desire to recover, to find a space within and without, where she could sustain the will to be well and create affirming habits of being. *The Salt Eaters* begins with a question, asked by the elder black woman healer. She says to Velma, who has tried to kill herself and is barely alive, "Are you sure, sweetheart, that you want to be well?" Only an affirmative response makes healing possible. In her introduction to the recently published collection of essays *The Black Women's Health Book: Speaking for Ourselves,* Evelyn White reminds readers of the grim statistics that document the grave health problems facing black women. Significantly, she reports that "more than 50 percent of black women live in a state of emotional distress." This will surprise few black women, who are daily assaulted by institutionalized structures of domination that have as one of their central agendas undermining our capacity to experience well-being.

In the Sisters of the Yam support groups, which continued for years, we found that one important source of healing emerged when we got in touch with all the factors in our lives that were causing particular pain. For black females, and males too, that means learning about the myriad ways racism, sexism, class exploitation, homophobia, and various other structures of domination operate in our daily lives to undermine our capacity to be self-determining. Without knowing what factors have created certain problems in the first place we could not begin to develop meaningful strategies of personal and collective resistance. Black female self-recovery, like all black self-recovery, is an expression of a liberatory political practice. Living as we do in a white-supremacist capitalist patriachal context that can best exploit us when we lack a firm grounding in self and identity (knowledge of who we are and where we have come from), choosing "wellness" is an act of political resistance. Before many of us can effectively sustain engagement in organized resistance struggle, in black liberation movement, we need to undergo a process of self-recovery that can heal individual wounds that may prevent us from functioning fully.

In *Sisters of the Yam: Black Women and Self-Recovery*, I want to share those strategies for self-recovery that I and other black women have used to heal our lives in Sisters of the Yam support groups and elsewhere. Though I write about the healing process as an individual, the insights shared are collective. They emerge from my lived experience of community and communion with black people. Even though our collective healing as a people must be a collective process, one that includes black men, I speak here directly to black women because I am most familiar with the issues we face.

Often when I tell black folks that I believe the realm of mental health, of psychic well-being, is an important arena for black liberation struggle, they reject the idea that any "therapy"—be it in a self-help program or a professional therapeutic setting—could be a location for political praxis. This should be no surprise. Traditional therapy, mainstream psychoanalytical practices, often do not consider "race" an important issue, and as a result do not adequately address the mental-health dilemmas of black people. Yet these dilemmas are very real. They persist in our daily life and they undermine our capacity to live fully and joyously. They even prevent us from participating in organized collective struggle aimed at ending domination and transforming society. In traditional southern black folk life, there was full recognition that the needs of the spirit had to be addressed if individuals were to be fully self-actualized. In our conventional religious experience we sang songs that posed profound questions like: "Is it well with your soul? Are you free and

made whole?" Psychological problems were not ignored
back then. They were treated by the diverse and usually
uncertified "healers" who folks knew to take their troubles
to. In the years before television, folks talked to one
another. Conversation and story-telling were important
locations for sharing information about the self, for healing. Let us remember that psychotherapy is often called
the "talking cure."

Recently, I and the other guests on a talk show
focusing on the crisis in black family life exemplified by
domestic violence. We were asked to suggest strategies
that would help. I urged that black families talk more with
one another, openly and honestly. In his essay "Dying as
the Last Stage of Growth," Mwalimu Imara speaks about
the importance of open communication:

> We seldom think of conversation as commitment, but
> it is. I find that expressing what I really feel and
> telling another person what is actually important to
> me at the moment is difficult. It requires a commit-
> ment on my part to do so, and I sense that this is true
> for most of us. It is equally difficult to listen. We are
> usually so full of our own thoughts and responses that
> we seldom really listen close enough to one another to
> grasp the real flavor of what the other person is
> attempting to convey. Creative communication in
> depth is what allows us to experience a sense of
> belonging to others. It is the force that limits the
> destructive potential in our lives and what promotes
> the growth aspects. Life is a struggle. Coping with a
> lifetime of change is a struggle, but through a lifetime
> of change we will experience ourselves as full persons
> only to the degree that we allow ourselves that com-
> mitment to others which keeps us in creative dialogue.

It is important that black people talk to one another,
that we talk with friends and allies, for the telling of

our stories enables us to name our pain, our suffering, and to seek healing.

When I opened my tattered copy of *The Salt Eaters* today, I found these words written in pencil on the back cover. They were spoken to me by a student seeking recovery: "Healing occurs through testimony, through gathering together everything available to you and reconciling." This is a book about reconciliation. It is meant to serve as a map, charting a journey that can lead us back to that place dark and deep within us, where we were first known and loved, where the arms that held us hold us still.

**Chapter 1**

# Seeking After Truth

*We have to consciously study how to be tender with each other until it becomes a habit because what was native has been stolen from us, the love of Black women for each other. But we can practice being gentle with each other by being gentle with that piece of ourselves that is hardest to hold, by giving more to the brave bruised girlchild within each of us, by expecting a little less from her gargantuan efforts to excel. We can love her in the light as well as in the darkness, quiet her frenzy toward perfection and encourage her attentions toward fulfillment...As we arm ourselves with ourselves and each other, we can stand toe to toe inside that rigorous loving and begin to speak the impossible—or what has always seemed like the impossible—to one another. The first step toward genuine change. Eventually, if we speak the truth to each other, it will become unavoidable to ourselves.*

—Audre Lorde, "Eye to Eye," *Sister Outsider*

Healing takes place within us as we speak the truth of our lives. In M. Scott Peck's popular discussion of a new healing psychology in *The Road Less Traveled*, he emphasizes the link between dedication to truth and our capacity to be well. He stresses that: "One of the roots of mental illness is invariably an interlocking system of lies we have been told and lies we have told ourselves." Commitment to truth-telling is thus the first step in any process of self-recovery. A culture of domination is necessarily a culture where lying is an acceptable social norm. It, in fact, is required. White folks knew that they were lying about African slaves who labored from sun-up to sundown when they then told the world that those same slaves were "lazy." White supremacy has always relied upon a structure of deceit to perpetuate degrading racial stereotypes, myths that black people were inferior, more "animalistic." Within the colonizing process, black people were socialized to believe that survival was possible only if they learned how to deceive. And indeed, this was often the case.

Slaves often told "lies" to white oppressors to keep from being brutally punished or murdered. They learned that the art of hiding behind a false appearance could be useful when dealing with the white master and mistress. Skillful lying could protect one's safety, could help one gain access to greater resources, or make resistance possible. Slave narratives testify that the ability to deceive was a requirement for survival. One collection of slave narratives edited by Gilbert Osofsky is even titled *Puttin' on Ole Massa.* In her slave narrative *Incidents in the Life of a Slave Girl,* Harriet Jacobs expresses motherly pride that her children learn at an early age that they must keep the secret of her hiding place from oppressive white people as well as untrustworthy black folks. A Jamaican proverb that was often quoted among slaves urged folks to "play fool, to catch wise." This was seen as essential for black survival, even if it required lying and deceit.

Any reader of slave narratives knows that religious black folks expressed anger and rage that they were forced by oppressive social circumstances to commit the sin of "lying." Slaves expressed righteous indignation that oppressive white people created a dehumanizing social structure where truth-telling could be valued but not practiced and where black people were judged inferior because of their "inability" to be truthful. Caught in a double-bind, on one hand believing in the importance of honesty, but on the other hand knowing that it was not prudent to always speak truthfully to one's oppressors, slaves judiciously withheld information and lied when necessary. Even free black people knew that white supremacist power could so easily be asserted in an oppressive way, that they too practiced the art of hiding behind a false appearance in the interest of survival. In *The Narrative of Lunsford Lane,* published in 1848, Lane stated that even after freedom:

> I had endeavored to conduct myself as not to become obnoxious to the white inhabitants, knowing as I did their power, and their hostility to the colored people...First, I had made no display of the little property or money I possessed, but in every way I wore as much as possible the aspect of slavery. Second, I had never appeared to be even so intelligent as I really was. This all colored in the south, free and slaves, find it particularly necessary for their own comfort and safety to observe.

The realities of daily life in white-supremacist America conveyed to black people in the long years after slavery had ended that it was still not in their interest to forsake this practice of dissimulation. Continued racial oppression, especially when it took the form of lynching and outright murder of black people, made it clear to all black folks that one had to be careful about speaking the truth to whites.

Paul Laurence Dunbar's much quoted poem gives eloquent witness to how conscious black folks were of the way that they had to practice falsehood in daily life:

*We wear the mask that grins and lies,*
*It hides our cheeks and shades our eyes,*
*This debt we pay to human guile;*
*With torn and bleeding hearts we smile,*
*And mouth with myriad subtleties.*
*Why should the world be over-wise,*
*In counting all our tears and sighs?*
*Nay, let them only see us, while*
*We wear the mask.*

The justification for "wearing a mask" is obvious when we consider the circumstances of living in conditions of legal racial apartheid, where black folks had so little recourse with which to address wrongs perpetrated against them by whites. Yet the time has come when we must examine to what extent the practice of dissimulation, of being deceitful, carried over into our social norms with one another. Encouraged to wear the mask to ensure survival in relation to the white world, black folks found themselves using strategies of dissimulation and withholding truth in interpersonal relationships within black communities. This was especially true for gender relations.

Patriarchal politics not only gave black men a bit of an edge over black women, it affirmed that males did not have to answer to females. Hence, it was socially acceptable for all men in patriarchal society (black men were no exception) to lie and deceive to maintain power over women. Just as the slaves had learned from their white masters the art of dissimulation, women learned that they could subvert male power over them by also withholding truth. The many southern black women who learned to keep a bit of money stashed away somewhere that "he don't know about" were responding to the reality of domestic cruelty and violence and the need to have means to escape. However, the negative impact of these strategies was that truth-telling, honest and open communication, was less and less seen as necessary to the building of positive love relationships.

Even though most black children raised in traditional southern homes are taught the importance of honesty, the lesson is undermined when parents are not honest. Growing up, many of us saw that grown folks did not always practice the same honesty they told us was so important. Or, many times, we would tell the "truth" only to be punished for such talk. And again, since racism was still the crucial factor shaping power relations between black and white people, there was still an emphasis on practicing dissimulation—one that persists in most black people's lives.

Many of the survival strategies that were once useful to black people, like dissimulation, are no longer appropriate to the lives we are living and therefore do us grave harm. Imagine, for example, this scenario: A black woman professor who has never completed her Ph.D. finds that in her daily life most folks she interacts with simply assume that she has this degree. She finds it easier not to explain. And indeed finds that she receives greater respect and recognition when folks see her as doctor so-and-so. Yet, there is a price she must pay for this deception—inner stress, fear of being found out, fear of losing the status she has falsely acquired. Now, one healthy response she could have had when she found that people accorded her greater respect when they assumed she had the degree would have been to use this information as a catalyst inspiring her to complete unfinished graduate work. We could all give countless examples related to jobs where black folks feel that the decks are stacked against us to begin with because of racism and therefore feel it is okay to lie about skills, experience, etc. Unfortunately such strategies may help one get jobs but the burden of maintaining deception may be so great that it renders individuals psychologically unable to withstand the pressure. Lies hurt. While they may give the teller greater advantage in one arena, they may undermine her well-being in another.

Cultivating the art of dissimulation has also created an over-valuation of "appearance" in black life. So much so that black children are often raised to believe that it is more important how things seem than the way they really are. If illusions are valued more than reality, and black children are taught how to skillfully create them even as they are simultaneously deprived of the means to face reality, they are being socialized to feel comfortable, at ease, only in situations where lying is taking place. They are being taught to exist in a state of denial. These psychic conditions lay the groundwork for mental stress, for mental illness. Dissimulation makes us dysfunctional. Since it encourages us to deny what we genuinely feel and experience, we lose our capacity to know who we really are and what we need and desire. When I can stand before a class of predominantly black students who refuse to believe that conscious decisions and choices are made as to what roles black actors will portray in a given television show, I feel compelled to name that their desire to believe that the images they see emerge from a politically neutral fantasy world of make-believe is disempowering—is a part of a colonizing process. If they cannot face the way structures of domination are institutionalized, they cannot possibly organize to resist the racism and sexism that informs the white-dominated media's construction of black representation. And, on a more basic level, they lack the capacity to protect themselves from being daily bombarded and assaulted by disenabling imagery. Our mental well-being is dependent on our capacity to face reality. We can only face reality by breaking through denial.

In Alice Walker's novel *The Color Purple,* Celie, the black heroine, only begins to recover from her traumatic experiences of incest/rape, domestic violence, and marital rape when she is able to tell her story, to be open and honest. Reading fictional narratives where black female characters break through silences to speak the truth of their lives, to give testimony, has helped individual black women take the risk to openly share painful experiences. We see examples of such courageous testimony in *The Black Women's Health Book.* Yet many black readers of Alice Walker's fiction were angered by Celie's story. They sought to "punish" Walker by denouncing the work, suggesting it represented a betrayal of blackness. If this is the way folks respond to fiction, we can imagine then how much harder it is for black women to actually speak honestly in daily life about their real traumatic experiences. And yet there is no healing in silence. Collective black healing can take place only when we face reality. As poet Audre Lorde reminds us in "Litany For Survival":

> *and when we speak we are afraid*
> *our words will not be heard*
> *nor welcomed*

*but when we are silent*
*we are still afraid*

*So it is better to speak*
*remembering*
*we were never meant to survive*

Collective unmasking is an important act of resistance. If it remains a mark of our oppression that as black people we cannot be dedicated to truth in our lives, without putting ourselves at risk, then it is a mark of our resistance, our commitment to liberation, when we claim the right to speak the truth of our reality anyway.

Many individual black women, particularly those among us involved in feminist movement, consider it important that black females who have been victimized by traumatic events like incest and rape speak openly about their experiences. Yet some are not necessarily committed to a philosophy of well-being dedicated to truth. While these individuals may applaud a black woman who publicly names an injury done to her by a man, they may fail to support her if she is committed to speaking truthfully in other areas of her daily life. These women may punish another black woman for speaking truthfully, or critique her by suggesting that she does not possess certain social graces. This is especially true among professional classes of black women who buy into notions of social etiquette informed by bourgeois values committed to keeping the public and the private separate. Indeed, black females from working-class backgrounds who have been raised to speak openly and honestly may find those traits a social handicap when dealing in bourgeois circles. They will be encouraged, usually by forms of social exclusion (which serve as punishment), to change their ways. It is not easy for a black female to be dedicated to truth. And yet the willingness to be honest is essential for our well-being. Dissimulation may make one more successful, but it also creates life-threatening stress.

Among poor and working-class black people the impetus to dissimulate is usually connected with the desire to cover up realities that are regarded as "shameful." Many of us were raised to be believe that we should never speak publicly about our private lives, because the public world was powerful enough to use such information against us. For poor people, especially those receiving any form of government aid, this might mean loss of material resources or that one's children could be taken away. Yet, again, we hold onto these strategies even when they are not connected to our survival and undermine our well-being. Telling the truth about one's life is not simply about naming the "bad" things, exposing horrors. It is also about being able to speak openly and honestly about feelings, about a variety of experiences. It is fundamentally not about withholding information so as to exercise power over others.

A few weeks ago, I was talking with one of my sisters about a very obvious lie that someone in our family had told to me. Emotionally upset, I was crying and saying, "I could deal with anything this family does if folks would just tell the truth. It's the lying that makes me feel crazy." We had a deep discussion about telling the truth, wherein she confessed that she tells a lot of lies. I was shocked, since I had always seen her as an honest person. And I wanted to know why. She admitted that it started with trying to gain a financial edge in her domestic life, but then she found herself just lying about little things even when it was not necessary. Analyzing this, we decided that the ability to withhold information, even it was something very trivial, gave her a feeling of power. We talked about the importance of learning that this feeling is "illusory" for it does not correspond with actual power to effect changes in one's daily social reality and is thus ultimately disenabling. Parents who lie do nothing to teach children the importance of speaking the truth.

For many poor black people, learning to be honest must take place in a situation where one also learns to confront the question of shame. The dominant culture acts as though the very experience of poverty is shameful. So how then can the poor speak about the conditions of their lives openly and honestly. Those of us raised in traditional southern black homes were taught to critique the notion of "shame" when it was evoked to strip us of dignity and integrity. We were taught to believe that there was nothing shameful about being poor, that richness of life could not ultimately be determined by our access to material goods. Black women working as maids in white homes had first-hand experience to prove money did not guarantee happiness, well-being, or integrity.

It is one of the tragic ironies of contemporary life that the privileged classes have convinced the poor and under-class that they must hide and deny the realities of their lives while the priveleged go public, in therapy, sharing all that they might have repressed out of shame, in order to try and heal their wounds. In the introduction to my third book, *Talking Back,* I wrote about the importance of speaking openly and honestly about *our* lives. I wrote about the negative "flak" I get from folks for being honest. Or lately, in bourgeois work settings, it is said about me that I do not keep confidences, when what is really happening is that I politically choose to resist being put in the position of keeping the secrets of the powerful, or of being welcomed into social circles of deceit. I had written years ago that "even folks who talk about ending domination seem to be afraid to break down the barriers separating public and private" by truth-telling. That still seems to be the case. Hence, it must be remembered that to be open and honest in a culture of domination, a culture that relies on lying, is a courageous gesture. Within white-supremacist capitalist patriarchal culture, black people are not supposed to be "well." This culture makes wellness a white luxury. To choose against that culture, to choose wellness, we must be dedicated to truth.

By giving up the illusory power that comes from lying and manipulation and opting instead for the personal power and dignity that comes from being honest, black women can begin to eliminate life-threatening pain from our lives. As I wrote in *Talking Back:*

> There are some folks for whom openness is not about the luxury of "will I choose to share this or tell that," but rather, "will I survive—will I make it through will I stay alive?" And openness is about how to be well and telling the truth is about how to put the broken bits and pieces of the heart back together again. It is about being whole, being wholehearted.

Many black women in the United States are brokenhearted. They walk around in daily life carrying so much hurt, feeling wasted, yet pretending in every area of their life that everything is under control. It hurts to pretend. It hurts to live with lies. The time has come for black women to attend to that hurt. M. Scott Peck ends his chapter "Withholding Truth" by reminding us that folks who are honest and open can feel free:

> They are not burdened by any need to hide. They do not have to slink around in the shadows. They do not have to construct new lies to hide old ones. They need waste no effort covering tracks or maintaining disguises...By their openness, people dedicated to the truth live in the open, and through the exercise of their courage to live in the open, they become free from fear.

In black life, the church has been one of the few places that has encouraged black folks to live truthful lives. Yet hypocrisy has come to be a central characteristic of the contemporary black church. The old black folks took the Biblical passage that declares "the truth will set you free" to heart. And, while the church might have changed, these words are still true. Their healing power can be felt in black women's lives if we dare to look at ourselves, our lives, our experiences and then, without shame, courageously name what we see.

# Chapter 2

# Tongues of Fire
## Learning Critical Affirmation

Writing about truth-telling in relationship to black experience is difficult. Making connections between the psychological strategies black folks have historically used to make life bearable in an oppressive/exploitive social context and then calling attention to the way these strategies may be disenabling now when we use them in daily life, particularly in intimate relationships, can too easily sound academic. I look back on the previous chapter and it does not read with the ease that I have become accustomed to in self-help books. Maybe this is why the self-help books we read rarely talk about political realities. I want to shift the tone now, however, and speak more concretely about how we confront issues of openness and honesty. Oftentimes, black folks find it easier to "tell it like it is" when we are angry, pissed, and desire to use "the truth" as a weapon to wound others. In such cases, even though a speaker may be open and honest, their primary agenda may be to assert power over another person and hence use the practice of truth-telling to assault someone else's psyche. That is why this chapter attempts to distinguish between the harsh critiques we give one another, which may contain "truth," and liberating truth-telling—they are not the same.

Raised in a family of sharp-tongued women, who were known to raise their voices, to argue and cuss, I and my five sisters learned early on how "telling it like is" could be used as a weapon of power to humiliate and shame someone. Here is an example from my experience. Growing up I was very skinny and saw this as a sign of extreme unattractiveness. Relentlessly teased by my sisters and my brother (who often told elaborate stories that entertained everyone about how often he had witnessed the wind blowing me away and had to chase after me and hold onto my feet to keep from losing me), my family completely reinforced the sense that to be skinny was to be ugly and a cause for shame. Now, whenever my family described me as skinny, they were being honest. Yet, what was the intent behind the honesty? Usually, it was to make me the object of ridicule and mockery. Though often the object of unkind "reading" that humiliated and shamed, I learned to protect myself by also developing the skill to name just that bit of information about someone that would expose them and make them feel vulnerable. What we all participated in was a practice of verbal assault, truth-telling as a weapon. In contemporary black culture this practice often takes the form of calling somebody out, that is "reading" them, or in a milder form, "dissin" them. Having someone critically analyze you and expose aspects of your reality you might like to keep hidden or deny, can be constructive and even pleasurable; however, it usually takes place in a context where the intent is to hurt or wound.

Exploring the way we as black women use this form of "telling it like is" will help some of us, who may see ourselves as open and honest, examine whether we are really dedicated to truth-telling when we are exposing something about someone else. Harsh criticism, with a truth-telling component, is often a major characteristic of black mother-and-daughter relationships. Since many black women were and still are raised in households where most of the love and affection we receive comes from black women elders—mothers, aunts, and grandmothers—who may also use criticism in a verbally abusive way, we may come to see such a practice as a caring gesture. And even though it wounds, we may imagine this hurting takes place for our own good.

Let me give an example that is fresh in my memory because it was a story told to me just yesterday by T., a young black woman. Attending a girlfriend's college graduation, she went out to eat with her friend's family. During dinner, the mother kept calling attention to the fact that her daughter needed to lose weight. Now it should be obvious that the public setting was not an appropriate place for such a dialogue. And why on a special day, a time when the daughter's achievements should be focused on and celebrated, does the mother call attention to perceived flaws or failings? When T. tried to intervene on her friend's behalf and assert that she thought she looked fine, she was kicked under the table by her friend and made to hush. Probably, like many of us, the friend is so accustomed to her mother choosing inappropriate moments to offer criticism, or always being critical, that she adjusts by simply not responding. For some of us, the endless negative critiques we have received from our mothers have been very disenabling. Yet, having learned how to use criticism with truth content to wound, we may employ the same practices. And like mothers who do this, when called on it, we may fall back on insisting that we are "just being honest." Here honesty is evoked to cover up abusive practices and hurting intent. This is not the kind of honesty that is healing. And it is vitally important for black female well-being that we can distinguish it from a commitment to truth-telling.

Often black females are raised in households where we are told by mothers who constantly give disparaging critiques, "I would be less than a mother if I did not tell you the truth." When trying to analyze the sources of this faulty logic, I trace it back, once again, to the survival strategies black folks developed to adjust to living in a white-supremacist context. The reality of racial apartheid was such that most black folks knew that they could never really trust that they would be "safe" in that white-dominated world outside the home or the all-black neighborhood. To gain a sense that they had some control over this situation, they set standards for behavior that were seen as appropriate safeguards. When racial integration happened, black folks did not immediately disregard these strategies, they adjusted them. One adjustment was the attempt to second-guess what the critical white world might say to disparage, ridicule, or mock and to prevent that from happening through self-critique and changing one's behavior accordingly. We were raised hearing stories about mothers punishing black children who were given no clear sense of what they had done that was considered wrong or inappropriate, because they felt that the child might assert themselves in ways outside the home that might lead white people to abuse and punish them. Setting up a system of internal checks required not only vigilant self-scrutiny, but also a willingness to place oneself in the mindset of the oppressor. This meant that black people were not focusing attention on constructing ways to critically affirm ourselves. Instead they worked at developing strategies to avoid punishment. Since no in-depth studies have been done looking at attempts on the part of black people to see ourselves through the negative eyes of the colonizer/oppressor, we can only speculate that such practices helped create a social climate where black folks could be harshly critical of one another. Living in a sexist society, where mothers are often blamed for any problem that arises with children, it makes sense that black mothers have often felt the need to assert control over their children in ways that are oppressive and dominating. How else can they "prove" to outside onlookers that they are good parents? The desire, of course, is to be beyond reproach.

Fierce parental critique and the threat of punishment is a strategy many black women use to assert their authority with children. One has only to observe black women parenting young children in public places. Often the children are spoken to harshly—bring your ass over here like I told you, sit your black ass down and shut up—not because the mother is angry at the children but because she desires them to behave "appropriately" in public settings. She wants to be perceived as a good parent. Notice though that being a good parent is made synonymous with the extent to which one is able to exercise control over a child's behavior. We would do well to connect this obsession with control to the strategies of domination white people have used, and still use, to maintain authority over us. We need to better understand how black folks who feel relatively powerless to control their destiny exercise negative power over one another in hierarchical settings.

The parent-child relationship in a culture of domination like this one is based on the assumption that the adult has the right to rule the child. It is a model of parenting that mirrors the master-slave relationship. Black parents' obsession with exercising control over children, making certain that they are "obedient" is an expression of this distorted view of family relations. The parents' desire to "care" for the child is placed in competition with the perceived need to exercise control. This is graphically illustrated in Audre Lorde's autobiographical work *Zami.* Descriptions of her childhood here offer glimpses of that type of strict parenting many black parents felt was needed to prepare black children for life in a hostile white society. Not understanding the way racism works as a child, the young Audre decides to run for sixth-grade class president. She tells the news to her mother only to be greeted with these furious words:

> What in hell are you doing getting yourself involved
> with so much foolishness? You don't have better sense
> in your head than that? What-the-france do you need
> with election? We sent you to school to work, not to
> prance about with president-this election-that. Get
> down the rice, girl, and stop talking your foolishness.

When Audre participates in the election anyway and comes home crying and emotionally crushed because she did not win, her mother responds with rage, striking a blow that Lorde remembers "caught me full on the side of my head." Then her mother says:

See, the bird forgets, but the trap doesn't! I warned you! What you think you doing coming into this house wailing about election? If I told you once I have told you a hundred times, don't chase yourself behind these people, haven't I? What kind of ninny raise up here to think those good-for-nothing white piss-jets would pass over some little jacabat girl to select you anything?

And the blows continued. Though Lorde's background is West Indian, northern, and urban, those of us growing up in the south confronted the same craziness in our parents. I can remember when my sister V. wanted to play tennis after the schools were racially integrated. Up until then our black schools did not have tennis teams. Our parents could not afford the necessary equipment, however, but rather than explain this, they criticized V. and made it seem that she had a problem for wanting to play this game. Often after such strange incidents, after maternal rage had subsided, we might be given a bit of tenderness, behavior that further reinforced the notion that somehow this fierce, humiliating critique was for our own good. Again these negative parental strategies were employed to prepare black children for entering a white-dominated society that our parents knew would not treat us well. They thought that by making us "tough," teaching us to endure pain with a stiff upper lip, they were ensuring our survival.

Knowing the concern and care that informs such behavior, and understanding it better when we grow older, often leads black women in adult life to imagine that our "survival" and the successes we have gained are indeed due to our having been forced to confront negative critique and punishment. Consequently it is often difficult for black women to admit that dominating mothers who used a constant barrage of negative verbal abuse to "whip us into shape" were not acting in a caring manner, even if they acted out of positive intent. When I "got grown" and had to cope with running my own household—keeping it clean, buying necessities, paying the bills—I began to look with awe at Mama, wondering how she found the time to take care of seven children, clean, shop, and cook three meals a day with very little help from our patriarchal father. Understanding these hardships made the constant harsh humiliating way she often spoke to us make sense. I find it easy to forgive that harshness, but I now can also honestly name that it was hurting, that it did not make me or my siblings feel securely loved. Indeed, I always felt that not behaving appropriately meant that one risked wrath and punishment, and more frighteningly, the loss of love.

It is important for black women engaged in a process of self-recovery to examine the way in which harsh critique was used to "check" and police our behavior so that we can examine the extent to which we relate similarly to others. When my siblings and I were children, we vowed that we would not yell at our kids or say mean things the way Mama and Daddy did. Yet, some of us have, unwittingly, broken that vow. Visiting one of my sisters and her family for the first time, I was shocked at the harsh negative manner she used when speaking to her children. It was so much like our childhood, only there was one difference, her children used the same "nasty" tone of voice when speaking to each other. When I gently called her on it and voiced my concern, she expressed surprise. Working all day and coming home to more work, she had not really noticed how she and the kids were talking to one another. To make my honest critique a constructive, caring one, I suggested that we do role playing with the kids after dinner—talking the way they talk to one another, then showing how it could be done differently. Rather than saying: "Sit your ass down. I ain't gon tell you no more," we practiced saying politely but firmly: "Would you please stop doing that and sit down?" At first the kids made fun of their Aunt Glo and her stories about "noise pollution" and how the way we talk to one another can hurt our hearts and ears, but we could all see and feel the difference. Critical affirmation emerges only when we are willing to risk constructive confrontation and challenge. What my sister found with her children was that if she spoke in a completely harsh humiliating manner she might indeed get a quicker response than when she made declarations with caring tones, but the effect of the latter was so much better. She improved the family well-being even though it required greater concentration and a little more time to frame responses in a caring way.

To heal our wounds we must be able to critically examine our behavior and change. For years I was a sharp-tongued woman who often inappropriately lashed out. I have increasingly learned to distinguish between "reading" and truth-telling. Watching my behavior (actually jotting down on paper how many negative critical comments I made in a day) helped me to change my behavior. Most black women know what it is like to bear the brunt of brutal tongue-lashings. Most of us have been told the "truth" about ourselves in ways that have been hurtful and humiliating. Yet, even so, many of us continue to see harsh critique as a means to strengthen character.

We need to know that constructive critical affirmation is just as effective a strategy for building character, if not more so. We find this out through an ongoing practice of critical affirmation. Often the harsh abusively critical voice-of-authority that we heard in childhood enters us. Then we no longer have to be in the presence of a dominating authority figure to hear that voice, for it speaks to us from within. In self-healing, black women can identify that voice within ourselves and begin to replace it with a gentle, compassionate, caring voice. When we see the positive results in our lives, we are then able to extend the generosity we give ourselves to others. Having silenced the negative voice within, and replaced it with loving caring criticism, it is also important for black women to practice speaking in a loving and caring manner about what we appreciate about one another. For such an action makes it evident to all observers of our social reality that black women deserve care, respect, and ongoing affirmation.

# Chapter 3

# Work Makes Life Sweet

"Work makes life sweet!" I often heard this phrase growing up, mainly from old black folks who did not have jobs in the traditional sense of the word. They were usually self-employed, living off the land, selling fishing worms, picking up an odd job here and there. They were people who had a passion for work. They took pride in a job done well. My Aunt Margaret took in ironing. Folks brought her clothes from miles around because she was such an expert. That was in the days when using starch was common and she knew how to do an excellent job. Watching her iron with skill and grace was like watching a ballerina dance. Like all the other black girls raised in the fifties that I knew, it was clear to me that I would be a working woman. Even though our mother stayed home, raising her seven children, we saw her constantly at work, washing, ironing, cleaning, and cooking (she is an incredible cook). And she never allowed her six girls to imagine we would not be working women. No, she let us know that we would work and be proud to work.

The vast majority of black women in the United States know in girlhood that we will be workers. Despite sexist and racist stereotypes about black women living off welfare, most black women who receive welfare have been in the workforce. In *Hard Times Cotton Mill Girls,* one can read about black women who went to work in the cotton mills, usually leaving farm labor or domestic service. Katie Geneva Cannon remembers: "It was always assumed that we would work. Work was a given in life, almost like breathing and sleeping. I'm always surprised when I hear people talking about somebody taking care of them, because we always knew that we were going to work." Like older generations of southern black women, we were taught not only that we would be workers, but that there was no "shame" in doing any honest job. The black women around us who worked as maids, who stripped tobacco when it was the season, were accorded dignity and respect. We learned in our black churches and in our schools that it "was not what you did, but how you did it" that mattered.

A philosophy of work that emphasizes commitment to any task was useful to black people living in a racist society that for so many years made only certain jobs (usually service work or other labor deemed "undesirable") available to us. Just as many Buddhist traditions teach that any task becomes sacred when we do it mindfully and with care, southern black work traditions taught us the importance of working with integrity irrespective of the task. Yet these attitudes towards work did not blind anyone to the reality that racism made it difficult to work for white people. It took "gumption" to work with integrity in settings where white folks were disrespectful and downright hateful. And it was obvious to me as a child that the black people who were saying "work makes life sweet" were the folks who did not work for whites, who did what they wanted to do. For example, those who sold fishing worms were usually folks who loved to fish. Clearly there was a meaningful connection between positive thinking about work and those who did the work that they had chosen.

Most of us did not enter the workforce thinking of work in terms of finding a "calling" or a vocation. Instead, we thought of work as a way to make money. Many of us started our work lives early and we worked to acquire money to buy necessities. Some us worked to buy school books or needed or desired clothing. Despite the emphasis on "right livelihood" that was present in our life growing up, my sisters and I were more inclined to think of work in relation to doing what you needed to do to get money to buy what you wanted. In general, we have had unsatisfying work lives. Ironically, Mama entered the paid workforce very late, after we were all raised, working for the school system and at times in domestic service, yet there are ways in which she has found work outside the home more rewarding than any of her children. The black women I talked with about work tended to see jobs primarily as a means to an end, as a way to make money to provide for material needs. Since so many working black women often have dependents, whether children or other relatives, they enter the workforce with the realistic conviction that they need to make money for survival purposes. This attitude coupled with the reality of a job market that remains deeply shaped by racism and sexism means that as black women we often end up working jobs that we do not like. Many of us feel that we do not have a lot of options. Of the women I interviewed, the ones who saw themselves as having options tended to have the highest levels of education. Yet nearly all the black women I spoke with agreed that they would always choose to work, even if they did not need to. It was only a very few young black females, teenagers and folks in their early twenties, who talked with me about fantasy lives where they would be taken care of by someone else.

Speaking with young black women who rely on welfare benefits to survive economically, I found that overall they wanted to work. However, they are acutely aware of the difference between a job and a fulfilling vocation. Most of them felt that it would not be a sign of progress for them to "get off welfare" and work low-paying jobs, in situations that could be stressful or dehumanizing. Individuals receiving welfare who are trying to develop skills, to attend school or college, often find that they are treated with much greater hostility by social-service workers than if they were just sitting at home watching television. One woman seeking assistance was told by an angry white woman worker, "welfare is not going to pay for you to get your B.A." This young woman had been making many personal sacrifices to try and develop skills and educational resources that would enable her to be gainfully employed and she was constantly disappointed by the level of resentment toward her whenever she needed to deal with social services.

Through the years, in my own working life, I have noticed that many black women do not like or enjoy their work. The vast majority of women I talked to before writing this chapter agreed that they were not satisfied with their working lives even though they see themselves as performing well on the job. That is why I talk so much about work-related stress in Chapter Four. It is practically impossible to maintain a spirit of emotional well-being if one is daily doing work that is unsatisfying, that causes intense stress, and that gives little satisfaction. Again and again, I found that many black women I interviewed had far superior skills than the jobs they were performing called for but were held back because of their "lack of education," or in some cases, "necessary experience." This routinely prevented them from moving upward. While they performed their jobs well, they felt added tension generated in the work environment by supervisors who often saw them as "too uppity" or by their own struggle to maintain interest in their assigned tasks. One white-woman administrator shared that the clearly overly-skilled black woman who works as an administrative assistant in her office was resented by white male "bosses" who felt that she did not have the proper attitude of a "subordinate." When I spoke to this woman she acknowledged not liking her job, stating that her lack of education and the urgent need to raise children and send them to college had prevented her from working towards a chosen career. She holds to the dream that she will return to school and someday gain the necessary education that will give her access to the career she desires and deserves. Work is so often a source of pain and frustration.

Learning how to think about work and our job choices from the standpoint of "right livelihood" enhances black female well-being. Our self-recovery is fundamentally linked to experiencing that quality of "work that makes life sweet." In one of my favorite self-help books, Marsha Sinetar's *Do What You Love, The Money Will Follow*, the author defines right livelihood as a concept initially coming from the teachings of Buddha which emphasized "work consciously chosen, done with full awareness and care, and leading to enlightenment." This is an attitude toward work that our society does not promote, and it especially does not encourage black females to think of work in this way. As Sinetar notes:

> Right Livelihood, in both its ancient and its contemporary sense, embodies self-expression, commitment, mindfulness, and conscious choice. Finding and doing work of this sort is predicated upon high self-esteem and self-trust, since only those who like themselves, who subjectively feel they are trustworthy and deserving dare to choose on behalf of what is right and true for them. When the powerful quality of conscious choice is present in our work, we can be enormously productive. When we consciously choose to do work we enjoy, not only can we get things done, we can get them done well and be intrinsically rewarded for our effort.

Black women need to learn about "right livelihood." Even though I had been raised in a world where elderly black people had this wisdom, I was more socialized by the get-ahead generation that felt how much money you were making was more important than what you did to make that money. We have difficult choices ahead.

As black females collectively develop greater self-esteem, a greater sense of entitlement, we will learn from one another's example how to practice right livelihood. Of the black women I interviewed the individuals who enjoyed their work the most felt they were realizing a particular vocation or calling. C.J. (now almost forty) recalls that generations of her family were college-educated. She was taught to choose work that would be linked with the political desire to enhance the overall well-being of black people. C.J. says, "I went to college with a mission and a passion to have my work be about African-Americans. The spirit of mission came to me from my family, who taught us that you don't just work to get money, you work to create meaning for yourself and other people." With this philosophy as a guiding standpoint, she has always had a satisfying work life.

When one of my sisters, a welfare recipient, decided to return to college, I encouraged her to try and recall her childhood vocational dreams and to allow herself adult dreams, so that she would not be pushed into preparing for a job that holds no interest for her. Many of us must work hard to unlearn the socialization that teaches us that we should just be lucky to get any old job. We can begin to think about our work lives in terms of vocation and calling. One black women I interviewed, who has worked as a housewife for many years, began to experience agoraphobia. Struggling to regain her emotional well-being, she saw a therapist, against the will of her family. In this therapeutic setting, she received affirmation for her desire to finish her undergraduate degree and continue in a graduate program. She found that finishing a master's and becoming a college teacher gave her enormous satisfaction. Yet this achievement was not fully appreciated by her husband. A worker in a factory, whose job is long and tedious, he was jealous of her newfound excitement about work. Since her work brings her in touch with the public, it yields rewards unlike any he can hope to receive from his job. Although she has encouraged him to go back to school (one of his unfulfilled goals), he is reluctant. Despite these relational tensions, she has found that "loving" her work has helped her attend to and transform previous feelings of low self-esteem.

A few of the black women I interviewed claimed to be doing work they liked but complained bitterly about their jobs, particularly where they must make decisions that affect the work lives of other people. One woman had been involved in a decisionmaking process that required her to take a stance that would leave another person jobless. Though many of her peers were proud of the way she handled this difficult decision, her response was to feel "victimized." Indeed, she kept referring to herself as "battered." This response troubled me for it seemed to bespeak a contradiction many women experience in positions of power. Though we may like the status of a power position and wielding power, we may still want to see ourselves as "victims" in the process, especially if we must act in ways that "good girls, dutiful daughters" have been taught are "bad."

I suggested to the women I interviewed that they had chosen particular careers that involved "playing hard ball" yet they seemed to be undermining the value of their choices and the excellence of their work by complaining that they had to get their hands dirty and suffer some bruises. I shared with them my sense that if you choose to play hardball then you should be prepared for the bruises and not be devastated when they occur. In some ways it seemed to me these black women wanted to be "equals" in a man's world while they simultaneously wanted to be treated like fragile "ladies." Had they been able to assume full responsibility for their career choices, they would have enjoyed their work more and been able to reward themselves for jobs well done. In some cases it seemed that the individuals were addicted to being martyrs. They wanted to control everything, to be the person "in power" but also resented the position. These individuals, like those I describe in the chapter on stress, seemed not to know when to set boundaries or that work duties could be shared. They frequently over-extended themselves. When we over-extend ourselves in work settings, pushing ourselves to the breaking point, we rarely feel positive about tasks even if we are performing them well.

Since many people rely on powerful black women in jobs (unwittingly turning us into "mammies" who will bear all the burdens—and there are certainly those among us who take pride in this role), we can easily become tragically over-extended. I noticed that a number of us (myself included) talk about starting off in careers that we really "loved" but over-working to the point of "burn-out" so that the pleasure we initially found dissipated. I remember finding a self-help book that listed twelve symptoms of "burn-out," encouraging readers to go down the list and check those that described their experience. At the end, it said, "If you checked three or more of these boxes, chances are you are probably suffering from burn-out." I found I had checked all twelve! That let me know it was time for a change. Yet changing was not easy. When you do something and you do it well, it is hard to take a break, or to confront the reality that I had to face, which was that I really didn't want to be doing the job I was doing even though I did it well. In retrospect it occurred to me that it takes a lot more energy to do a job well when you really do not want to be doing it. This work is often more tiring. And maybe that extra energy would be better spent in the search for one's true vocation or calling.

In my case, I have always wanted to be a writer. And even though I have become just that and I love this work, my obsessive fears about "not being poor" have made it difficult for me to take time away from my other career, teaching and lecturing, to "just write." Susan Jeffers' book, *Feel the Fear and Do It Anyway*, has helped me to finally reach the point in my life where I can take time to "just write." Like many black women who do not come from privileged class backgrounds, who do not have family we can rely on to help if the financial going gets rough (we in fact are usually the people who are relied on), it feels very frightening to think about letting go of financial security, even for a short time, to do work one loves but may not pay the bills. In my case, even though I had worked with a self-created financial program aimed at bringing me to a point in life when I could focus solely on writing, I still found it hard to take time away. It was then that I had to tap into my deep fears of ending up poor and counter them with messages that affirm my ability to take care of myself economically irrespective of the circumstance. These fears are not irrational (though certainly mine were a bit extreme). In the last few years, I have witnessed several family members go from working as professionals to unemployment and various degrees of homelessness. Their experiences highlighted the reality that it is risky to be without secure employment and yet they also indicated that one could survive, even start all over again if need be.

My sister V. quit a job that allowed her to use excellent skills because she had major conflicts with her immediate supervisor. She quit because the level of on-the-job stress had become hazardous to her mental well-being. She quit confident that she would find a job in a few months. When that did not happen, she was stunned. It had not occurred to her that she would find it practically impossible to find work in the area she most wanted to live in. Confronting racism, sexism, and a host of other unclear responses, months passed and she has not found another job. It has changed her whole life. While material survival has been difficult, she is learning more about what really matters to her in life. She is learning about "right livelihood." The grace and skill with which she has confronted her circumstance has been a wonderful example for me. With therapy, with the help of friends and loved ones, she is discovering the work she would really like to do and no longer feels the need to have a high-paying, high-status job. And she has learned more about what it means to take risks.

In *Do What You Love, The Money Will Follow,* Sinetar cautions those of us who have not been risk-takers to go slowly, to practice, to begin by taking small risks, and to plan carefully. Because I have planned carefully, I am able to finally take a year's leave from my teaching job without pay. During this time, I want to see if I enjoy working solely as a writer and if I can support myself. I want to see if (like those old-time black folks I talk about at the start of the essay) doing solely the work I feel most "called" to do will enhance my joy in living. For the past few months, I have been "just writing" and indeed, so far, I feel it is "work that makes life sweet."

The historical legacy of black women shows that we have worked hard, long, and well, yet rarely been paid what we deserve. We rarely get the recognition we deserve. However, even in the midst of domination, individual black women have found their calling, and do the work they are best suited for. Onnie Lee Logan, the Alabama midwife who tells her story in *Motherwit,* never went to high school or college, never made a lot of money in her working life, but listened to her inner voice and found her calling. Logan shares:

> I let God work the plan on my life and I am satisfied at what has happened to me in my life. The sun wasn't shinin' every time and moon wasn't either. I was in the snow and the rain at night by my lonely self...There had been many dreary nights but I didn't look at em as dreary nights. I had my mind on where I was going and what I was going for.
>
> Whatever I've done, I've done as well as I could and beyond...I'm satisfied at what has happened in my life. Perfectly satisfied at what my life has done for me. I was a good midwife. One of the best as they say. This book was the last thing I had planned to do until God said well done. I consider myself—in fact if I leave tomorrow—I've lived my life and I've lived it well.

The life stories of black women like Onnie Logan remind us that "right livelihood" can be found irrespective of our class position, or the level of our education.

To know the work we are "called" to do in this world, we must know ourselves. The practice of "right livelihood" invites us to become more fully aware of our reality, of the labor we do and of the way we do it. Now that I have chosen my writing more fully than at any other moment of my life, the work itself feels more joyous. I feel my whole being affirmed in the act of writing. As black women unlearn the conventional thinking about work—which views money and/or status as more important than the work we do or the way we feel about that work—we will find our way back to those moments celebrated by our ancestors, when work was a passion. We will know again that "work makes life sweet."

## Chapter 4

# Knowing Peace
## An End to Stress

*It is against blockage between ourselves and others—those who are alive and those who are dead—that we must work. In blocking off what hurts us, we think we are walling ourselves off from pain. But in the the long run, the wall, which prevents growth, hurts us more than the pain, which, if we will only bear it, soon passes over us. Washes over us and is gone.*

—Alice Walker, *The Temple of My Familiar*

When we live in peace, our lives are not tormented by the anguish of stress. So much of what has been said in the previous chapters about black women's lives should indicate that ours are far from peaceful. Stress is a hidden killer underlying all the major health problems black women face. Over-burdened and over-extended, stress is the body's response to carrying more than it can bear. When we are trying to do more than we can, confront more than we could possibly cope with in several lifetimes, we end up feeling that our lives are out of control, that we can only "keep a hold on life" by managing and controlling. Ironically, stress usually manifests itself most harmfully when things are out of control, yet many black women try to cope by attempting to assert and maintain control, which of course intensifies the stress. When we feel that we can no longer assert meaningful, transformative agency in our lives, when we are doing too much, when we experience an ongoing impending sense of doom, constant anxiety, and worry, stress has invaded our lives and taken over. Without our even knowing quite how it happened, we have forgotten what it feels like to live without debilitating stress.

Life-threatening stress has become the normal psychological state for many black women (and black men). Much of the stress black people experience is directly related to the way in which systems of domination—racism, sexism, and capitalism, in particular—disrupt our capacities to fully exercise self-determination. It is a tragic irony that many more black people suffer undue anxiety and stress as a result of racial integration. Elsewhere, I have talked about the fact that coming home to black neighborhoods that were not controlled by a visible white presence provided black people the necessary space to recoup and regain a measure of sanity. The power of these segregated communities was that they were places where black folks had oppositional world views that helped us sustain our integrity, our very lives. There are many segregated communities still but they are not often constituted as communities of resistance. Now many black people work at jobs in integrated settings where the presence of racism may bring added tension to the work setting, and then we must encounter this same terrorizing tension in banks, stores, supermarkets, or public transportation. Many black people, especially the underclass and working poor, feel as though they are powerless to change most things in their lives. And yet they have to survive. They have to find the wherewithal to get up in the morning and make it happen. The whole process is profoundly stressful.

Since black women are major providers in black households, both in those where men are present and where they are not, we often feel it is up to us to keep it all together. If we examine the history of black women and work in this society, it clearly shows that we have been mostly employed in arduous, backbreaking jobs where we were forced to push ourselves way past normal limits. (Let us not forget that slavery was one ongoing work-until-you-drop system.) Black women then return home, to what sociologist Arlie Hochschild calls "the second shift," that is housework and childcare, usually without the help of male partners. The point I want to make is that black people, and black women in particular, are so well social-ized to push ourselves past healthy limits that we often do not know how to set protective boundaries that would eliminate certain forms of stress in our lives. This problem cuts across class. What's going on when professional black women who "slave" all day on the job, come home and work some more, then provide care and counseling for folks who call late into the night? Is it guilt about material privilege that makes us feel we remain "just plain folks" if we too are working ourselves into the ground even if we don't have to? Rarely are the statistics on heart disease, depres-sion, ulcers, hypertension, and addiction broken down by class so that we might see that black women who "have" are nearly as afflicted by these stress-related illnesses as those who "have not."

In a society that socializes everyone to believe that black women were put here on this earth to be little worker bees who never stop, it is not surprising that we too have trouble calling a halt. When my five sisters and I left home to set up our households, one of the first things we noticed about Mom was how she never stopped working. She was continuing a pattern set by her mother, who spent a lifetime getting up at the crack of dawn to begin the day's work. Mama's mother used to sell fishing worms and liked to fish herself. And I can remember them finding her when she was in her eighties where she had fallen down by the creek trying to dig worms and fish. In part, these generations of southern black people were so desperate to let the racist white world know that they were not "lazy" that they were compulsive about work. Had not slavery socialized the generations before them to be compulsive about work? Had not being farmers, working the land, meant long days of hard labor? The compulsive need we see in our Mom always to be busy, never to be resting (she has high blood pressure) is disturbing. And yet many of us have adopted a similar life pattern. We do not know when to quit.

Knowing when to quit is linked to knowing one's value. If black women have not learned to value our bodies then we cannot respond fully to endangering them by undue stress. Since society rewards us most, indicates that we are valuable, when we are willing to push ourselves to the limit and beyond, we need a life-affirming practice, a counter-system of valuation in order to resist this agenda. Most black women have not yet developed a counter-system.

Work-related stress is most often the manifestation of stress that is easiest to identify, even though it is not always the easiest arena to change. One of the original Sisters of the Yam left Yale as a lawyer and went to work in what appeared to be a marvelous job, one that was engaged in progressive social and political issues. Everything about this job seemed perfect for her needs. Yet, she has had to cope with disrespectful white supervisors who have not unlearned their racism. Most black women have horrendous stories about how white people continue to think we are working as their "maids," irrespective of our job status. Rather than being a space of empowerment, this job setting has been disenabling (my girl has aged— the stress she is experiencing shows in her face and her body language). Now nothing that has been disenabling and disheartening has been related to her job duties directly, it's all stress around interpersonal dynamics. Though she knows she must seek another job, financial concerns keep her working in a context that fundamentally assaults her well-being. Together, we have tried to think of strategies to lessen the stress and intensify her sense of agency. Her experience is similar to that of many black women.

Growing up, 1 heard the black women in our family who worked as maids talk about the stress of being constantly watched by white employers and I hear myself articulating that same annoyance when I am in the English department at my job. Unless black women begin to make our health, and our well-being, a central priority, we cannot begin to develop lifestyles that enhance our lives. This is not a simple task; but it is a rewarding one. In the future, I hope black women all around the United States will set up work-related support groups where someone with the skill and know-how can advise individuals about ways that they could re-map or change their ways of life and work patterns. I find that I am often better able to give clear advice to someone other than myself, so I think it's good to find a mutual acquaintance or friend to exchange constructive "reads" on one another's lives or work situation.

I suggested to the Yam lawyer whose work situation I described earlier that she spend some time visualizing what she would do at her job if her supervisors were not present, locating both how she would feel and ways she would work. Then I encouraged her to use this as a way to set agendas that do not allow her to become unduly distracted by interpersonal tensions. This exercise was directed at helping her get in touch with her power and agency in the work setting. The intent was to redirect her attention away from the problem and focusing instead on her ability to take specific actions on her own behalf. This is only a short-term solution, of course. She needs to leave this job. Time and time again I find myself saying to myself and to black women friends who make excuses to justify not leaving stressful jobs: "If the job is killing you, then you are not really enriching your life in any way by staying in it." My experience of black women friends and acquaintances indicates that those of us who stay in jobs that are "killing" us tend to feel compelled to create reasons for our actions, like over-spending (which then makes stress around finances and makes us need the job).

Practically every black woman I know spends way too much of her life-energy worried and stressed out about money. Since many of us are coming from economic backgrounds where there was never enough money to make ends meet, where there was always anxiety about finances, we may have reached adulthood thinking this is just the way life is. Concurrently, in such environments we may never have learned how to manage finances. Even though many of us go on to make incomes that far exceed those of the families we come from, we may over-extend through spending or sharing with friends and family and find that we do not have enough, that we are constantly in debt (which only intensifies stress). We need more black female financial advisers who can help sisters get it together and teach us how to use our money wisely. We need to know how to eliminate the stress around money in our lives.

Early on in my adult life, I found myself in debt because of clothing purchases. I had just finished college and was looking for a job and thought I needed a new wardrobe. One outfit would not do. The stress of this debt was so intense that I thought "never again." I began to read self-help books that inform readers how to manage money. In a short period of time, I was able to pay my debts and learn how to manage finances. Freeing my life of financial stress gave me yet another space to feel inner peace. And I have tried to share with other black women the strategies I used. Some of them are so convinced that it is impossible to eliminate financial stress that they refuse to really try. It is not impossible.

Of course, one of the simplest strategies to use is learning to live within one's means. That's hard because most of us desire things well beyond our means. Yet, we need to get a grip on what we spend money on. To do this one might record for a week, or a month, where one's money goes and to look at that as a map and analyze it. I find that too large a portion of my income is spent on telephone bills. Living in an isolated setting, I often rely on talking to friends and comrades for psychological support. But to eliminate one area of stress by creating another is problematic. I decided that it was important for me to keep calls within a set limit. To this end I now record each call, and what I think it costs, so I know when I'm reaching the limit. I used to say to friends (and still do when I don't stay within my set budget) that I can gauge what my mental state has been over the course of months by looking at my phone bills. Hearing this as commentary on my well-being, I began to think that maybe I needed to change location. When black women find ourselves (and many of us do) living away from community, from friends and family, to work "good" jobs, and then use the phone to have that community, we may need to evaluate whether or not we are gaining in overall quality of life by being where the "good" job is rather than where our love and support is.

Going against the grain, choosing community over a "good" job may be a hard choice for individual black women to make. Again, we are only able to make lifestyle choices that enhance well-being and reduce or eliminate debilitating stress if we believe we deserve to live well. Most black women do not have this sense of "entitlement." We are not raised to believe that living well is our birthright. Yet, it is. We have to claim this birthright. Doing so automatically creates a change in perspective that can act as an intervention on the stress in our lives. Accepting that we are entitled to live well, we feel empowered to make changes, to break with old patterns. This does not mean that we will not have to cope with difficulties that arise when we make changes. Quitting stressful jobs is often easier to do than charting new journeys, finding different maps that if followed will lead us to those locations of wellness.

For some of us, stopping a stressful work pace may mean confronting "voids" in our lives, areas of lack, unfulfillment, loneliness, and sorrow. Opal Palmer Adisa's essay "Rocking in the Sunlight: Stress and Black Women" (published in *The Black Women's Health Book*) addresses the stress black women feel when we are just downright dissatisfied with life. Adisa writes:

> Did you ever wonder why so many sisters look so angry? Why we walk like we've got bricks in our bags and will slash and curse you at the drop of a hat? It's because stress is hemmed into our dresses, pressed into our hair, mixed into our perfume and painted on our fingers. Stress from the deferred dreams, the dreams not voiced; stress from the broken promises, the blatant lies; stress from always being at the bottom, from never being thought beautiful, from always being taken for granted, taken advantage of; stress from being a black woman in white America. Much of this stress is caused by how the world outside us relates to us. We cannot control that world, at times we can change it but we can assert agency in our own lives so that the outside world cannot over-determine our responses, cannot make our lives a dumping ground for stress.

Positive thinking is a serious antidote to stress. Since so much of our personal worrying has to do with feeling that the worse that can happen will, we can truly counter this negative by changing thought patterns. This is not an easy task for many black people. Some of us (myself included) have been really "into" the cynical "read" on life. We express a lot of our negative thinking in humorous vernacular speech. It often has a quality of magic and sassiness that comforts. It's tied up with our sense of being able to look on the rough side and *deal*. Frankly, I must confess, it's been really, really hard for me to give up this habit of being and engage in positive thinking. The vast majority of black people, particularly those of us from non-privileged class backgrounds, have developed survival strategies based on imagining the worst and planning how to cope. Since the "worst" rarely happens, there is a sense of relief when we find ourselves able to cope with whatever reality brings and we don't have to confront debilitating disappointment.

Positive thinking feels a whole lot more scary. To think that the universe is not an alien place, that there are enough resources to meet everyone's needs—for a lot of us that smacks of not facing reality, and we pride ourselves on not being "pollyannas," most crudely as not being "white girls." Well, growing up my folks called me "miss white girl." Their nicknaming me this was very much related to the fact that I wanted what I wanted and when I did not get it I expressed my disappointment. I cried; I whined. They saw this as a sign of weakness and I internalized that thinking. Now I know better. Not being addicted to being tough, to facing everything with no show of hurt or pain, allows us to express disappointment, hurt, outrage, and be comforted. Bottling up emotions intensifies stress. In *The Salt Eaters,* when Velma's husband goes to masseuse Ahiro for his usual massage, he is stunned when he is told that what he needs is a good cry, that he should "never be too tired to laugh or too grown to cry." It is healthy to give expression to a wide range of emotions.

This a form of positive thinking and action that can dramatically reduce stress.

Black folks fear that too much positive thinking is unrealistic. And yet we can't really name the benefits of negative thought patterns other than warding off disappointment. What would it mean for black people to collectively believe that despite racism and other forces of domination we can find everything that we need to live well in the universe, including the strength to engage in the kind of political resistance that can transform domination? The messages of hope that were projected by Martin Luther King were important because he knew that through the difficult times there had to be a positive foundation to sustain the impetus to struggle and sacrifice. No wonder the last piece of writing he did, published after his death, is called *A Testament of Hope*.

Many outstanding black political leaders have been positive thinkers. Shirley Chisholm's autobiography *Unbought and Unbossed* is a powerful example of the way one can use positive thinking to realize dreams. A role model for me because of her unshakable integrity, she wants readers to know that she "persisted in seeking this path toward a better world." Declaring her personal confidence she states: "My significance, I want to believe, is not that I am the first black woman elected to the U.S. Congress, but that I won public office without selling out to anyone." And who among her peers would have imagined that she would be the first black, the first woman presidential hopeful in the United States? Very few people achieve against the odds without learning how to think positively. Even though many of us know this we still find it hard to let go negative thought patterns.

The self-help book that really enabled me to rethink my attitudes about positive thinking was *Feel the Fear and Do It Anyway*. One insightful paragraph was especially helpful. It focused on worry. In response to critics who suggest to her that positive thinking is unrealistic, the author, Susan Jeffers, asserts:

> It is reported that over 90% of what we worry about never happens. That means that our negative worries have about a 10% chance of being correct. If this is so, isn't it possible that being positive is more realistic than being negative? Think about your own life. I'll wager that most of what you worry about never happens. So are you being realistic when you worry all the time?

Worry is another major cause of stress in black women's lives. Many of us worry because it allows us to imagine that obsessive constant thinking about something, fretting, means we are in control. Learning when to let go is crucial to reducing and eliminating stress. And often black women do feel that what we worry about "does happen." This means that what we need to consider is whether positive thinking can change the outcome of events. Certainly, stress does not empower us to handle whatever comes our way.

It's important for black women committed to self-recovery to survey our lives and honestly identify what causes us stress. Then we need to look for ways to cope and change. I suffer a lot from insomnia. It causes me stress because often after a sleepless night I have to carry on with the activities of the day as though I am not tired. Meditating helped me learn to relax so that I could enhance the chances that I would sleep the night through or, if not, experience my wakefulness unstressfully. It would be useful to black women to hear more from one another about the ways we change our lives to reduce and/or eliminate stress. Initially, we need to believe that it's possible. We need to consciously work against the cultural norms that would have us accept stress as the only way to live. So many stress-related diseases that black women suffer are connected to the heart. There is a quality of heartbrokenness in many of our lives. We need to reclaim our ability to live heart-whole, able to handle without stress whatever life brings our way.

# Chapter 5

# Growing Away From Addiction

Self-recovery is an idea most people know best from programs that focus on helping people break addictions, usually to substances. Though I first learned of this term in political writing about the issue of decolonization, I have found it meaningful to connect the struggle of people to "recover" from the suffering and woundedness caused by political oppression/exploitation and the effort to break with addictive behavior. In contemporary black life, disenabling addictions have become a dangerous threat to our survival as a people. Still many black people refuse to take addiction seriously, or if we accept the harm to individual and community that addictions cause, we may refuse to take seriously what it means to create an environment where people can recover. Increasingly, books about addiction are emphasizing that ours is a culture of addiction. As early as 1975, Stanton Peele explained:

> Addiction is not a chemical reaction. Addiction is an experience—one which grows out of an individual's routinized subjective response to something that has special meaning for him—something, anything, that he finds so safe and reassuring that he cannot be without it...We still find that we learn habits of de-

pendency by growing up in a culture which teaches a sense of personal inadequacy, a reliance on external bulwarks, and a preoccupation with the negative or painful rather than the positive or joyous. Addiction is not an abnormality in our society. It is not an aberration from the norm; it is itself the norm.

A culture of domination undermines individuals capacity to assert meaningful agency in their lives. It is necessarily a culture of addiction, since it socializes as many people as it can to believe that they cannot rely on themselves to meet even their basic human needs.

Considering the way black people have been socialized, from slavery to the present day, to believe that we can survive only with the paternalistic support of a white power structure, is it surprising that addiction has become so all-pervasive in our communities? It is no mere accident of fate that the institutionalized structures of white-supremacist capitalist patriarchy have created a modern society where the vast majority of black people live in poverty and extreme deprivation—most often with no hope of ever changing their economic status. Living without the ability to exercise meaningful agency over one's material life is a situation that invites addiction. Concurrently, addiction among black people who have high incomes, who are professionals, is often directly related to the stress and low self-esteem engendered by working in settings with white people who have not unlearned racism, and by the feeling that we cannot effectively confront life's difficulties.

I have witnessed first-hand the anguish of addicted beloved family members and experienced learning how to help without being co-dependent. Thus, I believe black people cannot collectively experience recovery if we continue to deny the experience of addiction. I want to explore the way the societal construction of black women as "mammies" and caretakers, and our acceptance of that role, makes us likely candidates for the role of co-dependent, enabling those around us to maintain addiction. When I look at black life historically, seeking explanations for our refusal to see "addiction" as problematic, I find again and again, especially among the underclass and working poor, the belief that the daily hardships and sufferings black folks face can only be endured if mediated by a realm of pleasure, and that wherever and however we find a way to feel good is acceptable. Within the slave system, rare days of collective pleasure involved substance abuse. It makes perfect sense that in a society of domination, where black folks remain a majority of the oppressed and exploited, that folks will seek out those social mechanisms that enable them to escape, that they will look for ways to numb pain, to experience forgetfulness. (Among black people in South Africa, alcoholism ranks high on the list of life-threatening diseases/addictions.)

In many traditional black communities, folks believed that an alcoholic was a person who drank too much and could no longer exercise control over his or her behavior. People who were obviously dependent on drink who manifested no anti-social behavior were never identified as alcoholics. And even though there is greater understanding about the nature of substance abuse in many contemporary black communities, there is still the assumption that it is not a problem if the person does not exhibit any anti-social behavior. Drug addiction has been more readily accepted as "dangerous" because so often it leads to anti-social behavior. Generally, folks think of anti-social behavior as that which leads an individual to cause physical harms to others or to property.

There has been little publicly expressed concern about psychological abuse in black life. When structures of domination identify a group of people (as racist ideology does black folks in this society) "mentally" inferior, implying that they are more "body" than mind, it should come as no surprise that there is little societal concern for the mental health care of that group. Indeed, by perpetuating and upholding domination, society invests, so to speak, in the ill health of certain groups, all the better to oppress and exploit them. Internalizing racist thinking or attempting to cavalierly subvert it, many black people tend to see us as having an edge on "silly" white people who have all these mental health problems and need therapy. Our edge, our one claim to superiority, is supposedly that we do not suffer mental illnesses. Myths like this one make it nearly impossible for some black folks to face the fact that psychological dilemmas may be an important source of addictions.

One aspect of the myth of the "strong" black woman that continues to inform black women's self-concept is the assumption that we are somehow an earthy mother goddess who has built-in capacities to deal with all manner of hardship without breaking down, physically or mentally. Many black women accept this myth and perpetuate it. Providing a convenient mask, it can be the projected identity that hides addiction and mental illness among black women. To confront addiction in our lives, to engage in a process of self-recovery, black women must break through all the forms of denial that lead us to pretend that we are always in control of our lives, that we don't go "crazy," that we don't abuse substances.

Two addictions affecting black women, which may not be as evident as alcohol or drug abuse, are food addictions and compulsive shopping. Since constant consumerism is such an encouraged societal norm, it is easy for black women to mask addictive, compulsive consumerism that threatens well-being, that leads us to lie, cheat, and steal to be able to "buy" all that we desire. Concurrently, in black life "fat" does not have many of the negative connotations that it has in the dominant society. Though black women are the most obese group in this society, being overweight does not carry the stigma of unattractiveness, or sexual undesirability, that is the norm in white society. This means, however, that it is very easy for black women to hide food addiction. In our family, though it was a custom to ridicule individuals who ate compulsively, it was never seen as a serious problem. Often food-addicted individuals were children of alcoholics. Yet, growing up, no one made the connection between the two disorders. It has only been in recent years that research on addiction has clarified the connections between sugar consumption and other forms of addiction. Many black children in the drug or alcohol-addicted family setting consume massive amounts of sugar, physiologically paving the way for other addictions in the future.

As noted, addictions in black life are often connected to the desire to experience pleasure and escape feelings of pain. The book *Craving for Ecstasy* is a powerful exploration of the way these longings serve as a catalyst for addiction. Our longing for candy as children was totally connected to the desire for pleasure, and especially that form of pleasure that was connected to a sense of transgression or taboo. In Toni Morrison's novel *The Bluest Eye,* Pecola, the little black girl who is full of self-hate, who is the victim of incest rape, counters her sense of personal anguish and shame by eating candy. Fond of a candy that features a picture of a little white girl who symbolizes the goodness and happiness that is not available to her, Pecola's addiction to sugar is fundamentally linked to her low self-esteem. The candy represents pleasure and escape into fantasy:

> Each pale yellow wrapper has a picture on it. A picture
> of little Mary Jane, for whom the candy is named.
> Smiling white face. Blond hair in gentle disarray, blue
> eyes looking at her out of a world of clean comfort. The
> eyes are petulant, mischievous. To Pecola they are
> simply pretty. She eats the candy, and its sweetness
> is good. To eat the candy is somehow to eat the eyes,
> eat Mary Jane, Love Mary Jane. Be Mary Jane.

Eating has always been a central location of pleasure in traditional black folk life. It becomes an addiction when individuals seek through compulsive behavior to experience again and again comfort and fulfillment via the substance. Many black women living alone (both working professionals and unemployed women) often use food and drink as ways to reward and comfort. Often these activities take the place of emotionally nurturing connections with other individuals, connections that are absent.

Addictions often become central to black women's lives when we experience life-altering stress. The breakup of a relationship, the loss of a loved one, and an abrupt loss of employment are just a few examples of situations that can lead individuals to abuse substances in an effort to keep going in life when they may feel like stopping.

Tragically, the energy received from addictions is artificial and ultimately takes its tolls. One of my family members became addicted to alcohol and drugs at a moment in her life when she was finding it impossible to cope with parenting. As an addict, she was perceived as being "out of control" no longer a "good" parent and it was acceptable for her to abandon her children to the care of other family members. What struck me about this was the reality that no one would have shown her much sympathy or regard had she come to the family and said: "I am having a nervous breakdown, I can't deal with these children. I need some space to recover myself." These requests would have gone against the strong black woman norm. No doubt she would have been told to "get a grip," that "wasn't nobody gonna do her job for her" or "if you didn't wanna raise kids you should have thought of that before you had them." As preposterous as it may seem, I wonder to what extent debilitating "addiction" has allowed black females, particularly the underclass and working poor, to take needed time out. Unfortunately, when addiction is the reason for breaking down or opting out, circumstances do not enable the individual to be engaged in a constructive "healthy" process of recovery.

Negative attitudes towards therapy in black life may make it hard for individuals to seek mental health care when they need it and thus heighten the likelihood that they will seek "relief" via substance abuse. Often traditional black mothers are among the group of black people who are most adamantly opposed to individuals seeking therapy. Their resistance to therapy seems to be linked with the notion that if a child (young or adult) has a mental health problem, the mother will somehow be blamed or perceived as having failed in her job. Our mother has demonstrated a greater willingness to cope with the negative ravages of addiction than she has to confronting constructively and positively the implications of helpful therapy. She has internalized the culture's pervasive mind/body splits. To the extent that addictions can be viewed solely as physiological, the world of the psyche, of the psychological, can be ignored. Hence, black people can recognize the ravages of addiction but still maintain the myth that we are not suffering from psychologically-based illnesses. Perceiving addiction as only about the body, and not about the mind, we can act as though there is no need to seek a therapeutic environment to experience recovery.

When a family member of mine was struggling to cope with crack addiction, and went through a period when he was "clean," I kept encouraging him to consider talking to someone—therapist, minister, anyone—about the deeper issues that might be the underlying dilemmas promoting his addiction. He resisted any analysis that suggested his substance abuse might be connected to psychological dilemmas and unreconciled psychological pain. Tellingly, he has been able to maintain his addiction and his addictive lifestyle because of the enabling support of black women—lovers, friends, and relatives. They have functioned in a co-dependent manner. Understanding co-dependency is crucial for black female self-recovery, for this is a role we often unwittingly assume.

In her book *When Society Becomes an Addict,* Anne Wilson Schaef suggests that a major characteristic of co-dependents is that they "are devoted to taking care of others." Sound familiar? She furthers states that "co-dependents frequently have feelings of low self-worth and find meaning in making themselves indispensable to others." Over and over again in the preceding chapters, I have talked about the ways in which black women are socialized to assume the role of omnipotent caregiver and the way our passive acceptance of this role is a critical barrier to our self-recovery. Nowhere is this more evident than in the addictive relational matrix where we so often function as co-dependents.

Let me give an example of co-dependent behavior. Imagine a black mother who has broken through her denial and accepted that her adult child is a drug addict. Knowing this, and knowing that the individual is using, she may still give money for gas or other needs, filling in the gaps created when the user spends all their funds on the habit. Though she may pride herself on "not giving her hard-earned money to anybody to buy drugs," she may be unable to see her child's empty refrigerator without buying food, or paying the rent—all actions that may be enabling. Of course throughout this process she gets to reaffirm that she is needed, that the child (usually an adult who has never learned in home or school to make responsible decisions) could not survive without her.

Many black women have difficulty letting their children grow. They continue to treat them as dependents long after such treatment is appropriate. Those of us raised in traditional black homes have all heard the phrase, "You'll always be a child to me." It is a common refrain, whenever we attempt to establish our autonomy as responsible adults. In his work on addiction, Stanton Peele emphasizes the link between passive acceptance of authority, of coercive hierarchical domination, and addiction. Seeing addiction as "a manifestation of a need for external structure" in his book *Diseasing of Americans,* he examines the way families and schools are places that keep individuals dependent, teaching them that it is most important to obey orders. Much black parenting focuses on the assertion of authority through coercion and domination. Respect of elders is made synonymous with obedience. Peele asserts that: "Fear of the unknown and the unwillingness to give up sure sources of nurturance—these are the ingredients of addiction." Perhaps future research on black people and addiction will explore the connection between leaving home (especially for those raised in predominantly black settings) and the effort to cope with living and working in predominantly white settings and addiction. Concurrently, such research might focus on the relationship between repressive parenting in black life and addiction.

The more black women work on our self-recovery, increasing our self-esteem, ridding our lives of debilitating stress, rejecting the learned impulse to try and meet everyone's needs, the less we will be seduced into co-dependency. Increasingly, I meet individual black women who are entering recovery programs to confront addiction and transform their lives. This is a positive sign for all of us. Talking with black women who have been in recovery programs about the path that led them there, a common factor was insurmountable pain, usually from the break-up of a relationship or a trauma surrounding significant family members. One person whose father had just been institutionalized for life-threatening alcoholism and related illnesses was also grappling with being in a primary relationship with an addict. She did not want to end up reliving her childhood, becoming a hostage to the past, so she went to a recovery program. Several other black women talked about the way reading courageous writings by black women about abuse and recovery enabled them to feel that an alternative life was possible, that it was possible to heal. They too sought therapeutic help. Though a number of the black women I spoke with had worked through recovery programs that use the Twelve Step model, each spoke of the difficulty of attending meetings where few if any black people were present. They all agreed that support and affirmation for recovery does not need to come from someone who shares the same race or gender, but they also acknowledged that it was meaningful and especially affirming to be able to share the recovery process with folks like themselves. In the future, we will hopefully hear more from black women who have confronted addictions, who are fully engaged in recovery, and whose transformed lives are living testimony.

## Chapter 6

# Dreaming Ourselves
# Dark and Deep
## Black Beauty

*Where there is a woman there is a magic. If there is a moon falling from her mouth, she is a woman who knows her magic, who can share or not share her powers. A woman with a moon falling from her mouth, roses between her legs and tiaras of Spanish moss, this woman is a consort of the spirits.*

—Ntozake Shange, *Sassafrass, Cypress and Indigo*

In a space before time and words, the world was covered in a thick blanket of darkness. It was a warm and loving covering. Since it was hard for the spirits who inhabited this space to see one another they learned to live by and through touch. So if you were running around lost you knew you were found when arms reached out in that loving darkness to hold you. And those arms that held the spirits in that beautiful dark space before time are holding us still.

This is a little origin story I made up. I thought of it one day when I was trying to explain to a little brown girl where the babies lived before they were born—so I told her they lived in this world of loving darkness. I made up this story because I wanted this little brown girl to grow up dreaming the dark and its powerful blackness as a magic space she need never fear or dread. I made it up because I thought one day this little brown girl will hear all sorts of bad things about the darkness, about the powerful blackness, and I wanted to give her another way to look at it. I held her hand, just like my father's father, Daddy Jerry, a man who worked the land, who knew the earth was his witness, had once held my hand in the darkest of summer nights and taught me that the blanket of night I was scared of was really longing to be my friend, to tell me all its secrets. And I reminded her, as he reminded me way back then, that those arms that first held us in that dark space before words and time hold us still.

Traditionally, black folks have had to do a lot of creative thinking and dreaming to raise black children free of internalized racism in a white-supremacist society, a society that is everywhere everyday of our lives urging us to hate blackness and ourselves. When we lived in the extreme racial apartheid of Jim Crow, it seems black folks were much more vigilant because we could never forget what we were up against. Living in our own little black neighborhoods, with schools and churches, in the midst of racism, we had places where we could undo much of the psychological madness and havoc wreaked by white supremacy. If that white world told us we were dirty and ugly and smelled bad, we retreated into the comfort and warmth of our bathtubs and our beauty parlors and our homemade perfumes and reminded ourselves that "white folks don't know everything." We knew how to invent, how to make worlds for ourselves different from the world the white people wanted us to live in. Even though there was so much pain and hardship then, so much poverty, and most black folks lived in fear, there was also the joy of living in communities of resistance.

Long before racial integration fundamentally changed the nature of those communities, disrupting black folks' ability to be self-affirming, they sent into our all black world a powerful tool that would teach us to internalize racism, that would teach us all manner of ways to be unloving toward ourselves, that tool was television. Learning to identify with the screen images of good and bad, whether looking at Westerns or Tarzan movies, television was bringing into the homes of black people a message that we were inferior, a race doomed to serve and die so that white people could live well. Even with this dangerous enemy in their house, many black folks were vigilant enough to resist. They watched television with a critical eye. Mama and Daddy explained the cinematic racial politics that made it possible for one white man to slaughter a thousand Indians. But somehow the sixties came and brought with them the promise that racism was about to end and many black people began to imagine that they no longer had to be vigilant, that it was no longer important to create an oppositional worldview that would protect them from internalizing white racism. The old deeply felt belief that black folks should be ever suspicious of the motives and intentions of white folks was replaced with a rhetoric of love that suggested we were all the same. And even though many black people knew we were not the same, they pretended. It took them a while to see that loving white folks in a white-supremacist culture really meant that they could never love blackness, nor themselves. Internalized racism seems to have a greater hold on the psyches of black people now than at any other moment in history.

Unfortunately, it has become an obvious cliché for people to point to the fact that racism encourages black children, and black grown-ups, to be self-hating and have low self-esteem. Yet highlighting the problem never seems to go hand-in-hand with finding solutions. Not all black people hate ourselves or our blackness. We come from a long line of ancestors who knew how to heal the wounded black psyche when it was assaulted by white-supremacist beliefs. Those powerful survival strategies have been handed down from generation to generation. They exist. And though a working public knowledge of them has been suppressed, we can bring this old knowledge out of dusty attics, closets of the mind where we have learned to hide our ghosts away, and relearn useful habits of thinking and being.

Certainly the slaves understood better than anybody that to be able to love blackness in a white world they had to create images—representations of their world that were pleasing to the sensibilities and to the eye. So they made quilts and dolls and all kinds of images that gave them a loving mirror of blackness to look into and be renewed. The book *Stitching Memories: African-American Story Quilts* shows the picture of an old log cabin quilt made in the 1870s depicting familiar, caring images of black life. This quilt always seems to me to embody a black woman's dream of how life would be in freedom. For in the quilt there are all these neat little houses. And the black folks outside, women and men, are taking care of plants and trees. We would be searching forever if we wanted to gather all the loving images enslaved and newly freed black folks created to remind themselves of their beauty and dignity in a world where their humanity was assaulted daily.

Clearly, if black women want to be about the business of collective self-healing, we have to be about the business of inventing all manner of images and representations that show us the way we want to be and are. Within white-supremacist patriarchal society, it is very difficult to find affirming images of black femaleness. A few years ago, I went to live in a new place where I knew no one, so it occurred to me that I needed to surround myself with life-affirming images of black womanness in my home to have in my midst representations of a nurturing community. I was shocked by how difficult it was to find representations of us where our features were not crudely distorted or exaggerated. I was dismayed by how many paintings showed us without eyes, or noses, or mouths. And I began to wonder if these body parts are "forgotten" because they represent the unloved, unliked parts, because they takes us into the realm of the senses. The problem that I encountered was not a dearth of imagery, but a lack of appealing imagery. So what did I do? I went to the home of a girlfriend who had been making little brown dolls (she had to dye material to make colors that could convey the variety of our complexions), and she made me six girl dolls to represent me and my sisters. My Aunt Ellen made me a quilt, each piece a black female figure. I added to these the brown baby doll I first received as a girl (that of course I kept for the daughter I dreamed about having someday), and a host of other family objects, passed through the generations, so that the spirit in these things could welcome and take care of me in my new place.

Obviously, the dearth of affirming images of black femaleness in art, magazines, movies, and television reflects not only the racist white world's way of seeing us, but the way we see ourselves. It is no mystery to most black women that we have internalized racist/sexist notions of beauty that lead many of us to think we are ugly. In support groups like Sisters of the Yam, all over the United States, I have seen black females of awe-inspiring beauty talk about how ugly they are. And the media has bomdbarded us with stories telling the public that little black children (and we are talking here primarily about girl children) prefer white dolls to black dolls, and think that white children are cleaner and nicer. The white-dominated media presents this knowledge to us as if it is solely some defect of black life that creates such aberrant and self-negating behavior, not white supremacy.

Many black people have always known how to love ourselves, our blackness, in the midst of white supremacy, despite those among us who internalize racist thinking. So we must ask ourselves, what is happening now that so few black folks, especially young black people, are able to resist. To come up with answers, I think it is crucial that we look at black female experience. For if the majority of black children are being raised by black females then certainly how we perceive ourselves, our blackness, informs the social construction of our individual and collective identity.

Returning to the images of beautiful black females who perceive themselves as ugly, let's explore the origin of their self-contempt. Putting aside the general ways sexist thinking about females effects self-concept, any examination of the way many black women learn to think about our bodies at an early age will show where the internalization of negative thinking begins.

The first body issue that affects black female identity, even more so than color, is hair texture. There is a growing body of literature (essays by black women writers Pearl Cleage, Lisa Jones, myself, etc.) that discusses our obsession with hair. But I want to start with basics. How is it that little black girls learn (even before we know anything about racism) that our hair is a problem? Negative thinking about our hair is usually conveyed in the home by parents, other caregivers, and siblings. One aspect of white-supremacist thinking that seemed to take hold of the black psyche in the 20th century was the assumption that straight hair was better—that it was "good" hair. I would like to suggest that apart from the racist assumption that any attribute of whiteness was better than blackness, over-worked black women often found that it took less effort to daily groom straightened hair than hair in its natural state. Practically speaking, a lot of black women learned to prefer straightened hair, to see it as better, because it took less time. If we consider that this attitude about time and effort spent on body grooming is a response to oppressive/exploitative conditions (overwork) then why is it black females often have the same attitude when such conditions do not exist?

Is this another "survival strategy" carried over into contemporary black life that is no longer needed? Certainly, going out to work in a white world that has always been threatened by black people who appear to be decolonized has had a major impact on what black females choose to do with our hair. Nowadays, more black women are asserting their right to choose natural hairstyles (braiding, locks, twists, etc.). Their choices make it possible for all black women to consider wearing natural hair.

As grown-ups, many of us look back at childhood years of having our hair combed and braided by other black women as a moment of tenderness and care that was peace-giving and relaxing. This dimension of sharing in care of the black female self is necessary in our life and we should seize all opportunities to feel caring hands tending our hair. In a workshop with black women recently, where one of the women present was trying to decide whether to "process" her hair, I began to talk about the different feel of natural hair, raising the question of whether processed hair is inviting to the touch. As with other such group discussions, black women there began to insist that they did not like to have anybody touching their hair. Yet, when pressed to look at the origins of this "dislike," it was found to be rooted in fear that our hair is really not an aspect of our being that most of us see as related to bodily pleasure. I have written elsewhere in an essay on hair that many black women view their hair as a problem, or as one black woman put it, a "territory to be conquered." To enjoy black hair, such negative thinking has to be unlearned. And in part we begin to unlearn it by talking to ourselves differently about our hair.

When we allow ourselves to experience the sensual pleasures of various black hair textures (especially in its natural state), we unlearn some of the negative socialization we are bombarded with about black hair. Despite the raised consciousness of black people around the question of internalized racism, most black magazines still favor images of black women with long straight hair. Often, in advertisements the light-skinned woman with straight hair will be depicted as the female who has a partner or who is more sexually appealing. In my workshops, there are always black women who will say that they would like to wear their hair natural but that whenever the subject comes up they receive negative feedback from family and friends. And, of course, heterosexual black females must often get past the fear that men will not find them appealing if they do not have straightened hair. Is it not a gesture of self-worth to interrogate the possibility that a black male who does not like unstraightened hair may have his own low self-esteem issues, and that may be an indication that a sister interested in such a man needs to be looking elsewhere for affirmation?

When we accept that it is an expression of self-worth and self-care for black women to choose to wear natural hairstyles in a society that does not affirm our beauty, we learn to be more appreciative of those individuals who can support our choices. A few weeks ago, I was in an airport and a black man came up to me, pointed to my curly kinky natural hair, and said, "Like your hair, really looks good." And it shocked me to think that I am almost forty and that this was perhaps the only time in a public setting that I received affirmation for having natural, unruly hair. I am more accustomed to hearing remarks like, "You could be fine if you did something with that hair." Since many black women learned in childhood to associate getting our hair combed with a painful, negative process, we have to practice positive thinking about the time spent grooming our hair. We have to learn to enjoy the process.

In groups with black women where we talk about our bodies, it is clear that many of us were raised in home environments where we were taught that it was a sign of vanity (all the more if these were religious households) to be "too" concerned with body care. Those of us coming from large families without material privilege, with only one bathroom, with the high cost of water and all products associated with body care, were certainly made to feel that ours should be a utilitarian approach to the care of the self. Now, living as we do in a racist/sexist society that has, from slavery on, perpetuated the belief that the primary role black women should play in this society is that of servant, it logically follows that many of us internalize the assumption that we/our bodies do not need care, not from ourselves or from others. This assumption is continually reinforced in our daily lives. Care of the self begins with our capacity to tenderly and lovingly care for the body. Black women often neglect our bodies.

When I first suggested to a group of black women that it was important for us to be able to stand naked in front of mirrors and look at our bodies, express our care for them, and our recognition of their beauty, many of the individuals thought this was just nonsense. Yet, is it nonsense that black women are the most overweight group in this society, that more than half of the women suffering with AIDS are black, that this and other diseases that most afflict us (diabetes, hypertension, heart disease, and cancer) are related to diet, to the basic health of our immune systems? Louise Hay, in *You Can Heal Your Life* and in *The Aids Book,* shows the relation between basic care of the self and our overall well-being. Since many black women (myself included) allow ourselves to become

over-extended—working, meeting the needs of others—
we often do not take time for care of the self. And those
among us who have been socialized from childhood on to
feel that black women's "personal power" only comes
through serving others may have the most difficult time
learning to see that personal power really begins with care
of the self.

In the past few years of my life I have over-worked—
teaching, writing, traveling to give lectures, doing "home
psychoanalysis" for me and everybody else. When I begin
to look critically at how I was treating my body and health,
I decided to make changes. It helped that friends would
say to me, "Weren't you sick and exhausted when I saw
you this time last year?" Yet, when I tried to pull back from
obligations, often clearly stating to folks that I needed to
take care of myself and my health, I often found that
people responded with hostility and anger. It seemed to
me that if folks in this society have been socialized via
racism and sexism to see black women as existing to
"serve," it often follows that folks feel we should continue
to serve even if we are sick, weary, or even near death. My
mother has completely internalized the notion that her
value is completely tied to her capacity to serve others.
Though in constant poor health, she perseveres. My sisters and I have expressed our rage at her unwillingness
to take care of herself, her well-being, a central agenda for
life. Even though we are grown women who are working
to unlearn what I call "the black woman martyr syn-
drome," there is still the child within us that wants to see
her change so that we can feel that it is fine for us to make
these changes, that we have her approval.

When one of my sisters, who has a husband and family, began to place "care of the self" on her agenda, her changes were greeted with familial rage and hostility. Considering that it was her practice to rush home from work and without even taking a moment's rest to begin meeting the demands of everyone, particularly fixing meals, it is not surprising that it was a shock to the family system when she began to suggest that not only would it be a positive help to her if people would make their own meals, but that the kids would learn both a sense of autonomy as well as realize their capacity to take care of their basic needs. The hostile responses that greeted her attempt to change patterns are called, by Harriet Lerner in *The Dance of Anger,* "countermoves" or "change back" behavior: "Countermoves are the other person's unconscious attempt to restore a relationship to its prior balance or equilibrium, when anxiety about separateness and change gets too high." Lerner's book usefully suggests constructive ways to cope with changing life patterns in intimate relationships.

Overeating or eating the wrong type of food is one of the majors ways black women abuse our bodies. Feminist books on the issue of fat say very little about black women's bodies, though *Shadow on a Tightrope* addresses some aspects of black female social reality. Black women need to write more about our eating issues. As noted earlier, we often use food as solace and comfort, to give us the pleasure that we may not be experiencing in other areas of our lives. In part, black women cannot begin to take care of body weight issues until we begin to care in an overall way for the body. If we do not focus concern with body weight by first approaching the black female body with respect and care, we may choose ways to deal with weight that are ultimately destructive. In a sexist culture, one that continues to socialize women to worship the thin female figure, women whose bodies will never conform to this model must go against the culture's norms to develop positive body esteem. For black women who must also confront racist stereotypes that devalue us, the resistance must be even stronger.

It is difficult to feel good about one's body when most of the clothes that are available to women are created without the bodies of black women in mind. Choosing clothing that looks appealing on our bodies is another critical issue for black women. The world of fashion is as much informed by racist/sexist assumptions about beauty as any other aspect of contemporary life. Although there are more images of black women in fashion magazines than ever before, the fact remains that the bodies of these women rarely resemble in any way the actual bodies of most black women. Concurrently, clothes that are designed for thin, anorexic-like figures rarely look good on bodies that are larger. Many black women are large. And many big black women are often forced by the economics of fashion (large size clothing is often only sold in specialty shops, and costs more) to push their bodies into clothes that are too small. The recent fashion interest in "ethnic" clothing (fashions imported from Third World countries, places where the body is not perceived as solely thin) makes it more possible for large women to find interesting-looking clothing that suits their size and shape. Clothing for large women is also often more conservative and matronly looking. This poses problems for large young black females. Of course a creative answer to this is for us to create and design clothes that meet the needs of black bodies. Right now this is happening all around the United States. These clothes can often be found on display in black-owned businesses, or they may be sold on the street in urban areas. When clothing is made with the large black woman in mind she can adorn herself in ways that affirm and appeal. This enhances body self-esteem.

Another area of the black female body that receives little or no focus, but usually indicates the degree of body self-esteem, is the feet. Recent studies on women and shoes reveal that the majority of women in this society stuff their feet into shoes that are at least one size too small. Many black women have large feet and again find it difficult to find reasonably priced shoes. Yet even the black females among us who wear regular sizes also abuse our feet by stuffing them into shoes that are uncomfortable or too little. Since many black females have learned that it is not "bad" to have hurting feet, or even that this is the norm, such thinking has to be unlearned if we are to acknowledge that the happiness and comfort of one's feet in daily life are crucial to well-being. This unlearning can begin when we pay attention to our feet.

Take a week in your life and keep a foot notebook. How comfortable are your shoes? How do your feet feel at the end of the day? How often do you give your feet that special bath and massage? Do you wear the same shoes all the time? Answering these questions can indicate areas where changes are needed. Often black females will buy a number of poorly made, cheaper-priced shoes that are not really comfortable when we could buy one pair of really well-made, comfortable shoes. And since many of us have irregular size feet, we need to know that we can always have a pair of shoes made especially for our feet. This is also a dimension of care for the self.

One also cannot really talk about black female body self-esteem without talking about the politics of skin color, about the way internalized racism encourages and promotes self-hatred and/or self-obsession. A fair-skinned black female who may be able to feel that she is lovely and desirable because of her skin color may rely so much on looks to negotiate her way through daily life that she will not develop other areas of her life, like a grounded personality or her intellectual skills. She may become so obsessed with seeking constant affirmation of her "beauty" that she may learn no skills that would enable her to fully self-actualize. Concurrently, darker-skinned black females who internalize the assumption that dark is ugly and constantly assault themselves by inner negative feedback also cannot fully self-actualize.

This is tragic. Without a doubt, dark-skinned black females suffer the most abuse when black people internalize white-supremacist notions of beauty. I have asked beautiful dark-skinned sisters what they feel enables them to resist the socialization that would encourage them to see themselves as ugly. They all talk about going through a stage where they had to unlearn old negative ways of thinking about themselves and learn how to be positive. They talk about surrounding themselves both with friends and comrades who affirm their looks but also with pictures and other representations. For many black women, Tracy Chapman is an important pop culture icon, not only because her music is deep and compelling, but because she has broken new ground in representing a black beauty aesthetic that is rarely depicted positively in this society. To see her picture on album covers, billboards, posters, and in magazines affirms that one does not have to be light-skinned with straight hair and thin nose to be regarded as beautiful.

There is no mystery as to why after all these years of black resistance to white racism, skin-color politics continue to be a negative force in our lives. White-supremacist thinking about color is so embedded in every aspect of contemporary life that we are daily bombarded in the mass media with images that suggest blackness is not beautiful. When I first saw images of black woman Naomi Campbell years ago, I was thrilled. It was so exciting to see this fine sister with full lips and natural hairstyles in fashion magazines. Seeing her image then was empowering. But when I see her now, usually wearing a long blonde straight wig, or some other nonsense, I resent this distortion of her image.

Negative representations are fundamentally disenabling. We know that black children have tremendous difficulty feeling good about their looks. Consider, for example, the black female parent who contacts me after hearing me give a lecture on black identity and explains that she is having a problem with a black girl child who comes home from school and puts a yellow mop on her hair to pretend that she is blonde and has long lovely locks. The mother says: "Our household affirms blackness. We have positive art images. We make positive comments about black beauty. And yet she thinks only white skin and long hair is pretty." Looking at the mother's appearance, I see that she has dark skin and processed hair. Straightened black hair is not always an indicator of low self-esteem. Yet there is no getting away from the reality that in a white-supremacist culture, where all aspects of blackness are devalued, it remains a sign that suggests one has opted for a style that may reinforce the notion that straight is better. No matter how I feel about myself, when little black children see me wearing straight hair in a context where they have learned from dolls, from television, or from playmates, that kinky textured hair is a "problem," in their eyes my appearance reinforces the idea that straight is better, more beautiful. I encouraged the black mother who wanted to know what she could do to improve her child's self-esteem to take time to openly and honestly examine her own deep-seated attitudes about skin color and hair texture, to see if she was possibly communicating negative messages to the child by the way she constructs her own body image.

For it really does not matter how many positive images of blackness we surround ourselves with, if deep down we continue to feel bad about dark skin and kinky hair. In this case, I felt the mother could intervene on this situation by first making sure that her own body gestures were self-affirming. Then I suggested it was important to look whether or not her daughter had access to toys and books with diverse, affirming images of black children. I encouraged her to look critically at the racial politics of her child's school, to find out to what extent it was an environment that affirmed blackness. Often black parents send black children into predominantly white school settings and then express surprise when their child's black identity is not fully affirmed. Yet, such a context can only be affirming if it is non-racist. Finally, I encouraged this mother to listen carefully to the kind of comments her husband and other males made about female beauty, as well as other black female authority figures. When a child adores a grown-up who makes certain pronouncements about beauty, that may have greater impact on the child's consciousness than comments coming from folks who do not matter as much.

A beautiful dark-skinned girlfriend of mine shared with me recently that, even though she was raised in a household where people "talked that black is beautiful stuff," whenever her father or brothers expressed any opinion about a woman's attractiveness, they chose someone who was either white or fair-skinned. And even though they told her she was beautiful, she never believed them. She remembered the many times they would say (what we have all heard black folks who suffer from internalized racism saying), "She's pretty to be so black."

I think most black folks know the kind of changes that must take place if we are to collectively unlearn racist body self-hatred, yet we often do not practice what we know. This is the challenge facing us. How many black females seize the opportunity daily to say or do something in relation to another black female or male that aims to affirm blackness and subvert the usual racist ways of seeing the black body? If internalized racism enters the souls of black folks through years of socialization then we are not going to be rid of it by simply giving shallow expressions to the notion that black is beautiful. We must live in our bodies in such a way that we daily indicate that black is beautiful. We must talk about blackness differently. And we cannot do any of this constructive action without first loving blackness.

To love ourselves, our blackness, we must be constantly vigilant, working to resist white-supremacist thinking and internalized racism. For some of us, this means cutting down the number of hours we watch television so that we are not subjected to forms of subliminal socialization shaping how we see the world. It means searching for decolonized black individuals who by the way they live and work demonstrate their love of blackness, their care of the self. Our love of blackness is strengthened by their presence. It means cultivating nonblack allies who have worked to unlearn their racism. Black women's body esteem is strengthened by good nutrition, exercise, and positive thoughts affirming that we deserve to be well—that our bodies are precious.

# Chapter 7

# Facing and Feeling Loss

*Living a self-conscious life, under the pressure of time, I work with the consciousness of death at my shoulder, not constantly, but often enough to leave a mark upon all of my life's decisions and actions. And it does not matter whether this death comes next week or thirty years from now; this consciousness gives my life another breadth. It helps shape the words I speak, the way I love, my politic of action, the strength of my vision and purpose, the depth of my appreciation of living.*

—Audre Lorde, *The Cancer Journals*

A few years ago I decided to write a book on African-American ways of dying. I chose to call it *When I Die Tomorrow*. The title is from a spiritual from long ago that can be heard in these contemporary times if you listen to the black women's musical group Sweet Honey in the Rock. The lyrics I love to hear in this song exclaim: "When I die tomorrow, I will say to the Lord, 'Oh Lord you been my friend. Thank you Lord you been my friend.'"

I began thinking and writing about traditional African-American ways of dying when I left home and went to college. It became apparent that this new life I was living was not going to teach me anything about death and dying.

In it I would never be sitting near the bedside of someone close to death or see the dead lying still in a bedroom surrounded by caring onlookers. And in this life I would not be in people's homes and hear them talking about who died and how they died and when the funeral was going to be. Even though in this bourgeois world I had entered people were dying, it was a very hush-hush affair. Folks did not come back from burying the dead and talk about how the dead had been laid out—how they looked, what they were wearing, whether or not the service was moving. Death was a hidden and taboo reality. This distance from the dead and dying seemed to make a profound difference in the way people lived and treated one another.

When I first read Elisabeth Kubler-Ross' *On Death and Dying*, I thought that I was not learning anything there that I had not learned "down home" watching southern black people cope with death and dying. Growing up, I learned to respect the reality of dying, not to ignore or make light of it. Mama would tell us often that "life was not promised," teaching us to live in the here and now. At the same time, we learned that there was nothing to fear about death. Many of the songs we sang at church celebrated death and dying as a transitional state, taking a person from one realm of being into another. In the traditional world of black folk culture, death was a time for grieving and rejoicing. There was no attempt to mask grief or to pretend in any way that losing a friend or loved one was not a cause for anguish or sorrow. Death was one of the rare moments when it was socially acceptable for folks to let go emotionally, to break down and surrender to their grief. These healthy approaches to death and dying made it possible for black people to confront and cope with loss.

Since not nearly enough has been written about death and dying in black experience, we can turn to fiction and catch a glimpse of those habits of being. In Toni Morrison's novel *Song of Solomon,* the funeral service of Hagar is both a time of grief and rejoicing. Mother and grandmother come to mourn the death of their "child." The anguish Reba and Pilate feel is expressed by their plaintive cry for "mercy." The mourners accept this invitation to acknowledge their pain in the manner of call and response. When Pilate cries "mercy," they collectively say, "I hear you." They sing this song:

> *In the nighttime.*
> *Mercy.*
> *In the morning.*
> *Mercy.*
> *At my bedside.*
> *Mercy.*
> *On my knees now.*
> *Mercy. Mercy. Mercy. Mercy.*

After they acknowledge profound grief, after they mourn, they then celebrate all that was joyous about Hagar, the love they felt towards her, and this is the final message that they share, "She was loved."

Learning how to express and accept grief was absolutely essential for black people living in the midst of profound racial apartheid. Without adequate medical care, denied entry to segregated hospitals, black folks could not keep death at a distance. Although I grew up in the kind of black world where folks really seemed to live to be so old (it was as though there was no death), it was a world where even the longevity of lives served as a constant reminder that death could come at any moment, that one had to be ready. We sang songs that reminded us: "Hush, children. Hush, children. Somebody's calling my name. Oh, my Lord. Oh my Lordy, what shall I do? Soon one morn, death is gonna creep into my room. Soon one morn, death is gonna creep into my room. Oh my Lord, Oh my Lordy, what shall I do?" We lived knowing death was in our midst. And we learned to appreciate living well so that we could meet death ready to go.

Back then, it was customary for the dying to gather loved ones, to reconcile, to share parting messages. And folks knew that even after all life had gone from the body, it was still possible to sit with the dead and let them feel one's presence, one's love and regard. The traditional "wake" remains a ritual that keeps alive old time beliefs that care must continue even after the body passes. Many southern black people have held to the belief that a human being possesses body, soul, and spirit—that death may take one part even as the others remain. In Patricia Jones-Jackson's study of traditions on the Sea Islands, *When Roots Die,* she discusses this concept of a tripartite self, sharing these words of a very religious man: "Listen to me good now: When you die in this world, you see, the...the...the...soul of a man go home to the Kingdom of God, but your spirit's still here on earth." Jackson reports that: "The spirit of one's ancestors is considered the closest link to the spirits of the 'other' world. Thus on the Sea Islands, as well as in Africa, spirits are asked to intervene on behalf of a living relative." What she describes are some of the secrets of healing that traditional black people kept alive and used in healing processes that could be labeled "psychoanalytical." The purpose was to understand complex mysteries in daily life and to create ways to intervene and enhance health and well-being.

I call attention to the old African-American ways of dying because they are a rich legacy we can bring into the present. Some of us have never relinquished those cultural practices because we were taught that "a body that knows how to die well, will know how to live well." In our process of self-recovery, black women must learn how to face death and dying in a manner that enables us to restore and renew our spirits. We can learn from the old ways. Living as many of us do in communities where we are alienated from the world of the dead and dying, where times of mourning and grief are not seen as growth experiences, we are often overwhelmed when we confront death. In her essay "Speaking of Grief: Today I Feel Real Low, I Hope You Understand" (published in *The Black Women's Health Book*), Bridgett Davis shares the insights that emerged after her personal confrontation with grief after the tragic deaths of several family members:

> I believe that on some deeper level, black women are used to tragedy. We expect it. Death is not a stranger to our lives, to our worlds. We've lost our fathers to hypertension and heart attacks, our brothers to front-line battles in American wars, our husbands and lovers to black-on-black crime or police brutality, and our sons to drug-laced streets or upstate prisons. All this while grappling with the stress and burden of all that is black life in America: Babies born to babies, dehumanizing ghettos, inferior schools, low wages, on-the-job racism...the slow but steady death of our people. We are just used to pain.

Being "used to pain" does not mean that we will know how to process it so that we are not overwhelmed or destroyed by grief. Like many black folks facing death head-on in urban environments, Davis struggled in isolation. Just the pace of life in cities makes constructive prolonged mourning in the context of community nearly impossible.

Sharing with one another ways to process pain and grief, black women challenge old myths that would have us repress emotional feeling in order to appear "strong." This is important because bottled-in grief can erupt into illness. Jeffers reminds us in *Feel the Fear and Do It Anyway* that: "Acknowledgment of pain is very important; denial is deadly." Describing the case of a woman who developed epilepsy after her son died, who opened herself to her grief nine years later, and found that her health miraculously improved, Jeffers shares, "Pain can be incredibly destructive if kept submerged...unacknowledged pain is subtly destroying many people's lives." Individual black women must ask ourselves, "Where are the spaces in our lives where we are able to acknowledge our pain and express grief?" If we cannot identify those spaces, we need to make them.

Starting a support group can be a helpful place. Let us imagine that D. is suffering from suppressed grief felt over the unexpected death of her mother. To all outsiders looking in, it appears that she has come to terms with this loss. In actuality, she thinks about her mother daily and feels deep down that her own life has somehow ended. If either D. or someone close to her gathered together a small group of folks, friends or acquaintances who may be grappling with grief in their lives, and started a support group focusing on loss, this setting could potentially be a place for healing. If D. continues to suppress her feelings, always hiding the fact that she feels her life has ended, she could enter a prolonged self-destructive depression.

There is not enough research about depression in black women's lives. How does it affect us? What can we do about it? In *Love, Medicine and Miracles,* Bernie Siegel makes a connection between depression and the breakdown of our immune systems that leads to illness:

> Depression as defined by psychologists generally involves quitting or giving up. Feeling that present conditions and future possibilities are intolerable, the depressed person 'goes on strike' from life, doing less and less, and losing interest in people, work, hobbies, and so on. Such depression is strongly linked with cancer.

Although depressed black females may completely withdraw in private life, in the public realm we will often continue to present a mask of "normalcy" even when we know we are suffering life-threatening "blues." Many of us suffer periods of suicidal depression that no one ever notices.

In black life, suicide, like so many other illnesses and behaviors related to the realm of psychological breakdown, tends to be seen as the gesture of a "weak" person. For years, many black people perpetuated and believed the myth that black folks did not commit suicide. That is a myth that is now brutally shattered by the overwhelming evidence that black folks—women, men, and children—are killing ourselves daily. Still, in a context where suicide is still seen as a sign of weakness, a character flaw, it is difficult for individuals to "confess" suicidal states and suicidal feelings.

Slightly more than a year ago, I was going through a tenure process at the college where I work. Being "judged" by my peers was a process that caused me great anxiety. I had many flashbacks to childhood, to being negatively judged in my family. During this time, I withdrew from colleagues. And, as is so often the case when people evaluate one another, this distance was more comfortable for both me and them. Often reassured that there would be no problems with the tenure decision, I felt silenced. I felt that I could not convey to anyone the tensions and terrors being in this position had evoked for me. And since I had ambivalent feelings about my job, I was also uncertain about what getting tenure would mean. I feared being locked into a comfortable job, a comfortable life that was not really good for me.

During this time, and even after the process was successfully completed, I had serious periods of depression, often feeling suicidal. Then, I would think if I killed myself it would be like all the other suicides of successful black women professionals—the people who knew me would say that I seemed all right, that they just didn't know I was having difficulties. Luckily for me, my sister V., who is a friend, comrade, and a therapist, was someone that I could share my feelings with. I went to stay at her place for a month, "chilling out," and doing what I call "home psychoanalysis." Together, we looked at the messages we received in childhood that might be making it difficult for me to accept "success." She gave me an exercise to do that was really helpful (one she had learned from a self-help book). In two paragraphs I was to describe what I would like my life to be like ten years from now. It took several weeks for me to complete the paragraphs but they conveyed to me that I really did have more of a "grip" on what I wanted than I had previously seen. This experience affirmed for me the importance of not suppressing suicidal feelings.

Like other black professional women who live alone and work in predominantly white settings, I am deeply disturbed whenever I hear that a sister/comrade in a similar situation has committed suicide. I felt this way when the Chicago journalist Leanita McClain killed herself at the age of thirty-two. In a long article about Mc-Clain, "To Be Black, Gifted, and Alone" black woman writer Bebe Moore Campbell offered these explanations:

> As her personal desires eluded her and the values of her old and new worlds collided, close friends witnessed spells of hysterical crying, brooding silence, and mounting depression. She began stockpiling the potent antidepressant drug amitriptyline prescribed by her physician. For all of her accoutrements of professional success, McClain was as full of despair as any ghetto dweller. On the night of what would have been her tenth wedding anniversary, McClain swallowed a huge overdose of amitriptyline and left both worlds behind.

Reading all the material I could find about McClain, both her writings and the commentary on her by others, I felt enraged at both the simplistic analysis that was often given to explain her death and the tacit acceptance of her fate that subtly implied her dying was inevitable. Writers suggested loneliness (not having a man), job stress, and alienation were all the reasons behind her suicide. And while these obvious reasons made sense, there was no attempt made in any writing I read to look at her childhood and make connections between that experience and her adult life. *A Foot in Each World*, the collection of her writings published after her death, was introduced by her

ex-husband and colleague who testified that "she constantly lamented to me and other close friends that life for
her no longer had much meaning." Clearly, many people
knew that McClain was in crisis. I ask myself again and
again why no meaningful life-sustaining intervention took
place. Could it be possible that, within the context of
white-supremacist capitalist patriarchy, McClain's "pain"
was taken for granted, that some people may have unconsciously perceived and accepted it as the "deserved punishment" a black woman gets when she pushes against set
boundaries and excels against the odds? Where was the
circle of love that could have embraced and held her while
she surrendered to the grief and pain that was within her?
Why was there no healing place?

Recently, hearing of yet another black woman whose
death had been declared a suicide, I once again thought
about the absent circle of love, the lack of a healing place.
Many of the same reasons that were given for McClain's
suicide were evoked in this case. And I thought, well, if I
had killed myself two years ago, people would say this
same shit: "She didn't have no man. She was lonely. She
was having trouble relating on the job." I could hear them
dredging up the gossip about affairs here and there that
did not work out. And I do not think any of these issues,
no matter how real they are in my life, would have been
accurate or adequate explanations. The "depression" I was
feeling was engendered by my need to be creatively challenged in life. Having reached a point where I was successfully completing a number of desired goals, I was
experiencing both a "void" and undergoing the kind of
critical self-examination that brought about a crisis in
meaning. It was a time for me to re-vision my life and chart

new and different journeys. I think it's very hard for successful black women (and black men) to turn away from achievements, high-status positions with visibility, that may no longer be meeting our growth needs.

What would have happened had McClain said to folks that despite all her success she really needed to change everything in her life—that she needed to start over. Writing "The Middle-Class Black's Burden" in 1980, McClain shared:

> I am burdened daily with showing whites that blacks are people. I am, in the old vernacular, a credit to my race. I am my brother's keeper, and my sister's, though many of them have abandoned me because they think that I have abandoned them. I run a gauntlet between two worlds, and I am cursed and blessed by both. I travel, observe, and take part in both; I can also be used by both. I am a rope in a tug of war. If I am a token in my downtown office, so am I at my cousin's church tea. I assuage white guilt. I disprove black inadequacy and prove to my parents' generation that their patience was indeed a virtue.

However much she may have "gloried" in her success, in the power of her achievements, McClain also knew that they took a psychological toll daily. Would her life have ended differently if she had known a wise Sister of the Yam who could have shared the critical insight that remaining always in a stressful position, walking a tightrope, is not good for the soul, that to live well and remain in this position one must take time out to nurture and renew the spirit, to unwind, relax, and recover? Would she have listened to wise Sisters of the Yam tell her: "Girl, you burning out—you need a change?" And would she have received unequivocal support from colleagues and loved ones if she had announced, "This has been a great journey but its time for me to travel a different road?"

In my own life, I have found that announcing the need for change has usually led others to point out how successful I am, and ask why I shouldn't pause just when I have gathered a certain momentum. They also frequently ask, "What will we do without you?" The support I have received has come from Yams, from therapeutic sessions with friends and counselors, who have been able to hear my pain, who have been willing to listen and hear me say that I enjoy my successes and at the same time I am in need of a change. Since my sister V. has also been re-mapping her life, first questioning whether a new job was really what she would like to be doing and then leaving the high-powered administrative position, we are able to give each other positive feedback for taking risks and comfort when we make mistakes.

Unreconciled grief, sadness, and feeling that life has lost meaning are all states of being that lead black women into life-threatening depression. Loss is no respecter of age. Very young children suffer debilitating depression. This is all the more likely if they are living in an abusive dysfunctional family. For some grown black women, the depressions we face can be traced back to childhood roots. Some of us hold our pain through years and years, letting it trouble our health. It would help contemporary black women to re-institutionalize meaningful death and dying rituals that older generations used that promoted healthy processes of grief, which taught us when and how to let go. All change can create sadness. It's when the sadness lingers that we can become stuck, mired, and unable to move. To the extent that black women are able to grapple with the larger reality of death and dying, we are better able to confront and cope with ongoing life-changes; we can move on. In the essay "Dying as the Last Stage of Growth," Mwalimu Imara argues that all change is a bit like dying: "Abandoning old ways and breaking old patterns is like dying, at least dying to old ways of life for an unknown new life of meaning and relationship. But living without change is not living at all, not growing at all. Dying is a precondition for living." With keen long-lasting insight, the ancestors were wise to teach us that "a body that knows how to die well will know how to live well." Collectively, black women will lead more life-affirming lives as we break through denial, acknowledge our pain, express our grief, and let the mourning teach us how to rejoice and begin life anew.

## Chapter 8

# Moved by Passion
## Eros and Responsibility

Reading black women's fiction we enter a world that unashamedly exposes the crisis in our "erotic" lives. That we have much to reconcile in relation to our sexualities and our sensualities is evident, whatever the sexual preference of the author. When I speak of eroticism here, it is not meant to evoke heterosexist images. I want to speak to and about that life-force inside all of us—there even before we have any clue as to sexual preferences or practices—that we identify as the power of the erotic. In her essay "Uses of the Erotic," Audre Lorde explains:

> The very word *erotic* comes from the Greek word *eros*, the personification of love in all of its aspects—born of Chaos, and personifying creative power and harmony. When I speak of the erotic, then, I speak of it as an assertion of the life-force of women; of that creative energy empowered, the knowledge and use of which we are now reclaiming in our language, our history, our dancing, our loving, our work, our lives.

Significantly, black lesbian women have been at the forefront of our efforts to transform black females' relationship to the erotic. Audre Lorde's powerful essay was groundbreaking. It not only provided us with a blueprint for rethinking the erotic away from the context of patriarchy and heterosexism, it gave us permission to talk publicly about sexual pleasure. Black lesbian writers like Diane Bogus share their efforts to understand the development of their erotic politics by re-examining childhood, their relationships within family. Bogus writes about her mother in the essay "Mom de Plume," sharing:

> So, I watched how you managed this married/single state. Unaware that you were sick and growing sicker, I saw you work full time, cook, clean, see after my brothers and men, and fill us with an indelible mother-wit. It is from here, then, that my nameless, boundless adoration, my emulation grew. Maybe during those few, but intensely loving, copyist years, I xeroxed a subliminal image of you which I have since applied towards my own happiness. Maybe, then, my lesbianism is no more than your manless self-reliance turned into itself.

By willingly, publicly, interrogating the realm of the erotic, black lesbian feminist thinkers paved the way for all black women to exercise our right to know and understand the erotic politically.

Concretely, lesbian, bi-sexual, and black female sex radicals challenge those black women trapped in the confines of a hurtful oppressive heterosexist eroticism to recognize that we have choices. In urging us to reconsider our relation to our bodies, as well as the bodies of other black women, the field of eroticism was expanded and with promise of greater passion and pleasure. These positive interventions are crucial. All our eroticisms have been shaped within the culture of domination. Despite our choices and preferences, we act in an erotic and liberatory way toward ourselves and others only if we have dared to break free from the cultural norms.

More than ever before in our history, black women are working to articulate an "erotic metaphysic" that can give direction and meaning to our experience. Borrowing this term from philosopher Sam Keen, who uses it in his work *The Passionate Life,* "an erotic metaphysic" evokes a vision of life that links our sense of self with communion and community. It is based on the assumption that we become more fully who we are in the act of loving. Keen elaborates: "Within the tradition of erotic metaphysics, which goes back to Augustine and Plato, love is assumed to be prior to knowledge. We love in order to understand." To think of an erotic metaphysics in black women's lives is to automatically counter that stereotype version of our reality that is daily manufactured and displayed in white-supremacist capitalist patriarchal culture.

Within a society where black women's bodies, our very beings, have been and are objectified in ways that deny our subjectivity, it has been incredibly difficult for black women to see the erotic as a space of power. Here it's important to distinguish the erotic from the sexual. Many black females learn early on how to objectify themselves, their bodies, and use their sexuality as a commodity that can be exchanged in the sexual marketplace. The black women who have internalized this way of thinking about their sexual selves, though they may appear "liberated," are in actuality completely estranged from their erotic powers. Their estrangement is just as intense as that of black females who have learned from childhood on that they can protect themselves from objectification, from commodification by repressing erotic energy, by denying any sensual or sexual dimension in themselves.

Just as breaking through denial is an initial stage in the healing process in other areas of our lives, it is equally true that black women will not be able to heal the wounded dimensions of our erotic lives until we assert our right to healing pleasure. Some of us are unable to imagine and create spaces of pleasure in our lives. When we are always busy meeting the needs of others, or when we are "used to pain," we lose sight of the way in which the ability to experience and know pleasure is an essential ingredient of wellness. Erotic pleasure requires of us engagement with the realm of the senses, a willingness to pause in our daily life transactions and enjoy the world around us. For many black females, the capacity to be in touch with sensual reality was perverted and distorted in childhood. Raised by authoritative coercive parents who were only primarily concerned with producing obedient children, many of us learned as little girls that we would always be punished for pleasure, for not keeping our clothes neat, for any small act of spontaneity that did not coincide with their objectification of us. We have all known black parents who treat girl children like "dolls" and expect them to behave as though they are puppets on a string performing on command.

These environments did not promote the development of creative imagination or affirm a child's desire to explore the world fully. Sam Keen reminds us that the world of the child at play is the foundation that can shape or misshape our ability to feel:

> In the play of the senses the child burrows beneath the boundaries of the persona. Touching, smelling,

> and tasting allow us to discover for ourselves if, and
> to what extent, the world makes sense. So long as we
> have bodies, we may retreat in to the sanctuary of
> experience. The senses are private oracles. When we
> consult them we discover a sacred bond that unites us
> to life.

For black children, this bond is often broken quite early. Many of us were made to feel as children that the world was completely unsafe, hence our capacity for wonder was repressed and fear took its place.

Touching as a way to experience reality was denied many of us as children. I was in a gift shop recently where a black child wanted to touch objects, to pick them up and look at them, the way other customers were doing. Her mother, however, kept insisting that she not touch anything, that if she did the people in the store might think she was stealing it. In so many public spaces, we can witness daily the way in which the curiosity of black children is suppressed. Taught not to reach out and touch objects in the world that invite interest and bring pleasure, many black children are socialized to think that this desire is "bad" and brings punishment. They learn to repress the desire to touch and the need to be touched. One of my sisters had to confront relatives who felt that she was touching her children "too much" and as a consequence was making them soft. Again the idea that black children must learn to be "tough" serves as the logic for denying them forms of physical bonding that communicate that their flesh is lovable, that it deserves tenderness and care.

Talking about ways individuals are rendered incapable of experiencing pleasure, Keen asserts: "Deprivation of bonding creates erotic poverty; erotic poverty gives rise to violence; violence further inhibits eros. We can't make love on a battlefield. The less care we receive, the less we are capable of giving." Young black females often learn early that they will not get any of their needs for physical touch and nurturance met in any realm except the sexual. There are few studies that look at the connection between early sexual experience, that may or may not lead to teenage pregnancy, and the desire to find a space where one can express the need to be touched. When black females have been deprived of emotional nurturance that includes touch at early ages, we may not know how to distinguish those longings from sexual desire. Not knowing the difference we may engage in early sexual encounters in an attempt to meet needs that are not sexual.

How many young black girls are able to articulate to partners they just need to be caressed, touched, or held? Does sex become the only way they can experience touch because they do not know how to ask? How many grown black females are fully able to acknowledge the healing power of touch? Are we touched enough? Do we give black children the touching they need? Many of us were raised to be embarrassed by physical displays of affection. In their autobiographical writings, black women often describe growing up in families where there were no physical expressions of care. In *Young, Gifted, and Black*, Lorraine Hansberry confessed that her family did not touch, did not ever even speak of love:

> If we were sick, we were sternly, impersonally and carefully nursed and doctored back to health. Fevers, toothaches were attended to with urgency and importance, one always felt *important* in my family. Mother came with a tray to your room with the soup and Vick's salve or gave the enemas in a steaming bathroom. But

we were not fondled, any of us—head held to breast, fingers about that head—until we were grown, all of us, and my father died. At his funeral I at last, in my memory, saw my mother hold her sons that way, and for the first time in her life my sister held me in her arms I think. We were not a loving people: we were passionate in our hostility and affinities, but the caress embarrassed us. We have changed little.

Many of us have had a similar experience. It is only when we leave home and return as adults that expressions of love seem possible. What is it about distance that enables us to acknowledge emotional need? Does the caress embarrass us because it serves as an active reminder that we are flesh and in need of tender loving care. Should we be surprised that a people whose bodies have been perpetually used, exploited, and objectified should now seek to turn flesh into armor?

When we consider the uses that this society has made of black women's bodies—as breeding machines, as receptacles for pornographic desires, as "hot pussies" to be bought and sold—surely our collective estrangement from a life-giving eroticism makes sense. Given the way patriarchy and notions of male domination inform the construction of heterosexual identity, the realm of black heterosexual sexual expression is rarely a place where black females learn to glory in our erotic power. Whereas black women's fictions narrate brutal destructive expressions of sexuality that mask themselves as desire between black men and women, black women's autobiographies rarely mention the realm of the sexual.

Paule Marshall's novel *Praisesong for the Widow* is unusual in its depiction of passionate lovemaking between a black man and woman that is rooted in mutual desire, in a shared longing to remain connected to creative black culture. Describing moments of sexual ecstacy that embrace this experience as sacred, Marshall writes:

> He would lie within her like a man who has suddenly found himself inside a temple of some kind, and hangs back, overcome by the magnificence of the place, and sensing around him the invisible forms of the deities who reside there: Erzulie with her jewels and gossamer veils; Yemoja to whom the rivers and seas are sacred; Oya, first wife of the thunder god and herself in charge of winds and rains...Jay might have felt himself surrounded by a pantheon of the most ancient deities who had made their temple the tunneled darkness of his wife's flesh. And he held back, trembling a little, not knowing quite how to conduct himself in their presence.

For Jay and Avey, sexuality is a place that allows them to recover themselves, to be more fully alive. Yet, Marshall depicts Jay as losing touch with his sensuality and his sexuality when he becomes overly obsessed with acquiring material goods, with gaining economic power. Marshall is one of the few black writers who shows a connection between advanced capitalism and black folks' consuming desire for goods that erases our will to experience the realm of the senses as a location of power and possibility.

If we listen to many contemporary black songs, rap and R&B, we can hear endless messages that make the space of erotic longing a site for exchange of goods, a site for the enactment of aggression. Listening to the pugilistic expression of sexual desire that is evoked in much male-centered rap music, we have to wonder what kind of sex young black people are having and ask ourselves why it is they connect sex with hostile aggressive acts, violence, even hatred. In white-supremacist culture, "blackness" is always made to be a sign of the anti-erotic. Whereas the black body may be sexualized, it is perpetually associated with negative sex thought (rape, disease). Fashion magazines tend to portray black women in ways that make their bodies appear "unnatural," mannequin-like, twisted out of shape. Often black females are displayed in pseudo street-corner style clothing (as though we are prostitutes), wearing straight wigs, and our features distorted. These sexualized images do not empower black women onlookers. Are they there for the voyeuristic white gaze, to render us as "objects" or possessions once again?

To see black female bodies as sacred is to counter the cultural insistence that they are worthless and expendable. Sacred bodies enter the realm of sexuality knowing how to give honor. Discussing the question of attitude in *The Art of Sexual Ecstasy,* Margo Anand reminds us that self-love enables us to experience pleasure, a sense of the ecstatic: "Love begins at home, with loving yourself. By this I don't mean self-centered indulgence, but the ability to trust yourself and to listen to you inner voice, the intuitive guidance of your own heart. Loving yourself means that you realize that you deserve the experience of ecstasy..." Many black women are struggling to accept and love our bodies. For some of us that means learning to love our skin color. Others of us may love our blackness but mentally mutilate, cutting the body into desirable and undesirable parts. In Toni Morrison's novel *Beloved,* Baby Suggs preaches a prophetic sermon in the midst of nature, in the woods, calling on black folks to love our flesh:

> "Here," she said, "in this place, we flesh; flesh that weeps, laughs; flesh that dances on bare feet in grass.

Love it. Love it hard. Yonder they do not love your
flesh. They despise it. They don't love your eyes; they'd
just as soon pick em out. No more do they love the skin
on your back. Yonder they flay it. And O, my people,
they do not love your hands. Those they only use, tie,
bind, chop off and leave empty. Love your hands! Love
them. Raise them up and kiss them. Touch others with
them, pat them together, stroke them on you face
'cause they don't love that either. You got to love it,
you!

Baby Suggs continues to name various parts of our
bodies calling us to love this flesh. For any black female
working on self-recovery issues around body esteem,
this would be a good meditation passage to read daily
for insight and reflection.

Loving our flesh, celebrating it, includes the eroticism of language, the way we talk to one another. So often,
we use harsh tones. We raise our voices. We forget how to
use black vernacular speech in a manner that consoles,
caresses, and delights. Yet, much more than standard
English, we can speak in dialect or patois to bring an aura
of pleasure and "down home" delight to our intimate
encounters. This is why Paule Marshall calls attention to
the way Jay and Avey talk to one another during lovemaking, engaging in a mutual dialogue of desire that intensifies their inter-subjectivity and diffuses the possibility
that they will become narcissistic and forget to recognize
one another. Dialogue is a powerful gesture of love. Caring
talk is a sweet communion that deepens our bonds. We can
show the depths of our care by the way we speak in all
areas of our lives, both public and private. Our words can
evoke the sense of respect and profound acknowledgment
of how precious we are to one another. Language can
convey a sense of the sacred.

Sacred sexuality begins when we touch our bodies in daily grooming. One of the truly special moments of tender caregiving occurs in *Praisesong for the Widow,* when Rosalie Parvey washes Avey's soiled body after she has made the difficult crossing to Carriacou. This bathing is ritualistic and healing. For black women it is an enchanting invitation to remember childhood baths when our bodies were touched and cleaned. It is a celebration of tender care that one black woman gives another even though they are strangers. In this twilight sensual space, Avey experiences a reawakening of her senses; she feels herself alive again to touch, smell, and sound: "She gave herself over then to the musing voice and to such simple matters as the mild fragrance of the soap in the air and the lovely sound, like a sudden light spatter of rain, as the maid wrung out the washcloth from time to time over the water in the galvanized tub." Shame about our bodies often prevents black females from giving one another affirmation and physical care. And then extreme homophobic fear continues to inform black people's inability to touch one another. Eradicating homophobia would allow us to embrace each other across sexual preferences without fear.

In the introduction to her new book of poems *The Love Space Demands,* Ntozake Shange speaks to the way in which fear of AIDS is leading some black folks to promote sexual repression: "Our behaviors were just beginning to change when the epidemic began, moving sex closer to shame now than anything since I've been alive. Words that undermine trust and liberty to feel are creeping back into the bedrooms and couches of our lives so that we are always second guessing each other." Margo Anand's book affirms that ecstatic sexual pleasure can be experienced within the context of safe sex. The AIDS crisis, which is affecting our communities greatly (more than 50 percent of the women with AIDS are black), has heightened our awareness that we can honor each other most in the context of shared eroticism by bringing to desire an openness and willingness to share in words who we are and what we have experienced as well as what we want, all without fear.

This should always have been a dynamic in healthy sexual experience. For many women, and in particular black women who have never been able to articulate their sexual fears, needs, or longings, it is difficult to engage in open discussion prior to a sexual encounter. This fear leads many heterosexual black women to accept being sexual without a condom, because they do not wish to initiate the discussion of safe sex with partners. A healing eroticism enables us to assume responsibility for articulating all our concerns whenever we are sexually interested and involved. Audre Lorde emphasizes that eroticism is frightening because it is life-affirming and calls us to resist any dehumanizing encounter. It is dehumanizing for women to submit to sex without condoms when they desire protection. As Lorde reminds us:

> For once we begin to feel deeply all the aspects of our lives, we begin to demand from ourselves and from our life-pursuits that they feel in accordance with that joy which we know ourselves to be capable of. Our erotic knowledge empowers us, becomes a lens through which we scrutinize all aspects of our existence, forcing us to evaluate those aspects honestly in terms of their relative meaning within our lives.

Empowered by a healing eroticism, black women are able to envision and engage in sexual encounters that do not diminish our well-being. A number of married black women that I spoke to talked about continuing to feel compelled to have sex with their partners against their will. We know that this gesture is dangerous for it demands that we suppress authentic feelings and pretend. That suppression alone acts to estrange us from our bodies, to alienate us from our needs, so that we lose touch. It must be resisted.

Since so many black women have experienced traumatic physical abuse; we come to sexuality wounded. Irrespective of our sexual preference, we need to be with partners who are able to hear us define boundaries and limits. We need partners who are able to give us the loving care that makes sexual healing possible. Those of us who have learned to openly and honestly name that we are abuse survivors find that our willingness to take care of ourselves invites reciprocal recognition and care from our sexual partners. Shange shares the insight in *The Love Space Demands* that "when we don't know what we mean or why we are doing what we do, we are only able to bring chaos and pain to ourselves and others." Keen, in *The Passionate Life*, calls us to enter sexual encounters with our whole selves in a different way, but his message is similar:

> A purely sensational approach to sex misses the paradox of pleasure. Human beings are not young forever, do not live in the perpetual moratorium of the game, and cannot isolate present sensations from associated feelings. We are multidimensional. Therefore pleasure is greatest when sensation (present awareness) feeling (past associations) and intentions (future expectations) are unified in a single whole. If all the parts of the self are allowed to participate, everything feels better.

At the core of an erotic metaphysics is the urgent call to know and love who we are so that we can become more fully ourselves in the space of passion and pleasure.

Black women are often more passionate in our rage and suffering than we are in our loving. The energy that we bring to situations that arouse hostility or pain can easily be redirected. We can tell ourselves daily to direct our most intense feeling to those areas of our lives that bring pleasure and delight. To achieve this end we need to write ourselves many recipes for tuning into healing erotic power and put them in a box so that when we see our energies going toward anger or suffering we can take a recipe from the box and follow it. When I am in pain or feeling sad, I am often unable to imagine what activities might create a shift in feeling. A box full of ideas can serve as a reminder. Singing, dancing, walking, or sitting meditation can all be used as a practice to bring us back in touch with our bodies. Learning to be still, in sitting meditation, is one way we can be one with our bodies. Buddhist monk Thich Nhat Hanh teaches that living in awareness, living mindfully, enables us to heal the wounded parts of ourselves. He encourages us to smile and smile often. We all know that black women often shut our faces down, turn them into impenetrable masks. Opening up our gaze is a gesture that can bring us closer to the outside world, making it more possible for us to experience joy and gratitude that we are alive, that we have another day on this earth in our bodies, that we can feel the body ecstatic.

As we attempt to envision a healing eroticism, Keen also encourages us to ask the question: "What forms of passion might make us whole? To what passions may we surrender with the assurance that we will expand rather than diminish the promise of our lives? Where may we look to catch a glimpse of the kind of passionate life that would heal both the psyche and the body politic?" These are important questions for black women seeking self-recovery. Those of us with feminist awareness find that the experience of passion in a non-sexist context is amazingly healing. Without knowing that we hold within ourselves so much fear, we find in encounters with one another, with caring partners, that sexuality has often been a fearful site but that it can be a place where we can let the fear go, where we can recover and come back to ourselves. We find that celebrating our union with the natural world and our natural selves awakens our senses and gives us pleasure. We find that there is a healing eroticism in liberation struggle when we actively engage every aspect of our being to bring to black experience beauty, honor, respect, and vigilant caretaking. Recovering a healthy passion, black women discover that we can pause in the midst of everyday activities and feel again the sense of wonder, of pleasure that we are flesh, that we are one with the universe, that there is a life-force within us charged with erotic power that can transform and heal our lives.

# Chapter 9

# Living to Love

Love heals. We recover ourselves in the act and art of loving. A favorite passage from the biblical Gospel of John that touches my spirit declares: "Anyone who does not know love is still in death."

Many black women feel that we live lives in which there is little or no love. This is one of our private truths that is rarely a subject for public discussion. To name this reality evokes such intense pain that black women can rarely talk about it fully with one another. *The Black Women's Health Book* had no chapter focusing specifically on love. And the only time the word was evoked in a chapter heading, it was in a negative context. The subject was domestic violence, the title "Love Don't Always Make It Right." Already, this title distorts the meaning of genuine love—real love does make it right. One of the major tasks black women face as we work for emotional healing is to understand more fully what love is so that we do not imagine that love and abuse can be simultaneously present in our lives. Most abuse is life-threatening, whether it wounds our bodies or our psyches. Understanding love as a life-force that urges us to move against death enables us to see clearly that, where love is, there can no disenabling, disempowering, or life-destroying abuse.

Because many black women make care synonymous with love, we confuse the issue. Care can take place in, for example, a familial context where there is also abuse, but this does not mean that love is present. In this chapter, I would like to offer ways to think about love that deepen our understanding of its meaning and practice. I want to shed light on the way our specific historical experience as black people living in a racist society has made it difficult and at times downright impossible for us to practice the act and art of loving in any sustained way.

It has not been simple for black people living in this culture to know love. Defining love in *The Road Less Traveled* as "the will to extend one's self for the purpose of nurturing one's own or another's personal growth," M. Scott Peck shares the prophetic insight that love is both an "intention and an action." We show love via the union of feeling and action. Using this definition of love, and applying it to black experience, it is easy to see how many black folks historically could only experience themselves as frustrated lovers, since the conditions of slavery and racial apartheid made it extremely difficult to nurture one's own or another's spiritual growth. Notice, that I say, difficult, not impossible. Yet, it does need to be acknowledged that oppression and exploitation pervert, distort, and impede our ability to love.

Given the politics of black life in this white-supremacist society, it makes sense that internalized racism and self-hate stand in the way of love. Systems of domination exploit folks best when they deprive us of our capacity to experience our own agency and alter our ability to care and to love ourselves and others. Black folks have been deeply and profoundly "hurt," as we used to say down home, "hurt to our hearts," and the deep psychological pain we have endured and still endure affects our capacity to feel and therefore our capacity to love. We are a wounded people. Wounded in that part of ourselves that would know love, that would be loving. The choice to love has always been a gesture of resistance for African-Americans. And many of us have made that choice only to find ourselves unable to give or receive love.

Our collective difficulties with the art and act of loving began in the context of slavery. It should not shock us that a people who were forced to witness their young being sold away; their loved ones, companions, and comrades beaten beyond all recognition; a people who knew unrelenting poverty, deprivation, loss, unending grief, and the forced separation of family and kin; would emerge from the context of slavery wary of this thing called love. Yet, some slaves must have dreamed that they would one day be able to fully develop their capacity to love. They knew first-hand that the conditions of slavery distorted and perverted the possibility that they would know love or be able to sustain such knowing.

Though black folks may have emerged from slavery eager to experience intimacy, commitment, and passion outside the realm of bondage, they must also have been in many ways psychologically unprepared to practice fully the art of loving. No wonder then that many black folks established domestic households that mirrored the brutal arrangements they had known in slavery. Using a hierarchical model of family life, they created domestic spaces where there were tensions around power, tensions that often led black men to severely whip black women, to punish them for perceived wrongdoing, that led adults to beat children to assert domination and control. In both cases, black people were using the same harsh and brutal methods against one another that had been used by white slave owners against them when they were enslaved. We know that life was not easy for the newly manumitted black slaves. We know that slavery's end did not mean that black people who were suddenly free to love now knew the way to love one another well.

Slave narratives often emphasize time and time again that black people's survival was often determined by their capacity to repress feelings. In his 1845 narrative, Frederick Douglass recalled that he had been unable to experience grief when hearing of his mother's death since they had been denied sustained contact. Slavery socialized black people to contain and repress a range of emotions. Witnessing one another being daily subjected to all manner of physical abuse, the pain of over-work, the pain of brutal punishment, the pain of near-starvation, enslaved black people could rarely show sympathy or solidarity with one another just at that moment when sympathy and solace was most needed. They rightly feared reprisal. It was only in carefully cultivated spaces of social resistance, that slaves could give vent to repressed feelings. Hence, they learned to check the impulse to give care when it was most needed and learned to wait for a "safe" moment when feelings could be expressed. What form could love take in such a context, in a world where black folks never knew how long they might be together? Practicing love in the slave context could make one vulnerable to unbearable emotional pain. It was often easier for slaves to care for one another while being very mindful of the transitory nature of their intimacies. The social world of slavery encouraged black people to develop notions of intimacy connected to expedient practical reality. A slave who could not repress and contain emotion might not survive.

The practice of repressing feelings as a survival strategy continued to be an aspect of black life long after slavery ended. Since white supremacy and racism did not end with the Emancipation Proclamation, black folks felt it was still necessary to keep certain emotional barriers intact. And, in the worldview of many black people, it became a positive attribute to be able to contain feelings. Over time, the ability to mask, hide, and contain feelings came to be viewed by many black people as a sign of strong character. To show one's emotions was seen as foolish. Traditionally in southern black homes, children were often taught at an early age that it was important to repress feelings. Often, when children were severely whipped, we were told not to cry. Showing one's emotions could lead to further punishment. Parents would say in the midst of painful punishments: "Don't even let me see a tear." Or if one dared to cry, they threatened further punishment by saying: "If you don't stop that crying, I'll give you something to cry about."

How was this behavior any different from that of the slave owner whipping the slave but denying access to comfort and consolation, denying even a space to express pain? And if many black folks were taught at an early age not only to repress emotions but to see giving expressions to feeling as a sign of weakness, then how would they learn to be fully open to love? Many black folks have passed down from generation to generation the assumption that to let one's self go, to fully surrender emotionally, endangers survival. They feel that to love weakens one's capacity to develop a stoic and strong character.

When I was growing up, it was apparent to me that outside the context of religion and romance, love was viewed by grown-ups as a luxury. Struggling to survive, to make ends meet, was more important than loving. In that context, the folks who seemed most devoted to the art and act of loving were the old ones, our grandmothers and great grandmothers, our granddaddys and great granddaddys, the Papas and Big Mamas. They gave us acceptance, unconditional care, attention, and, most importantly, they affirmed our need to experience pleasure and joy. They were affectionate. They were physically demonstrative. Our parents and their struggling-to-get-ahead generation often behaved as though love was a waste of time, a feeling or an action that got in the way of them dealing with the more meaningful issues of life.

When teaching Toni Morrison's novel *Sula*, I am never surprised to see black female students nodding their heads in recognition when reading a passage where Hannah, a grown black woman, asks her mother, Eva: "Did you ever love us?" Eva responds with hostility and says: "You settin' here with your healthy-ass self and ax me did I love you? Them big old eyes in your head would a been two holes full of maggots if I hadn't." Hannah is not satisfied with this answer for she knows that Eva has responded fully to her children's material needs. She wants to know if there was another level of affection, of feeling and action. She says to Eva: "Did you ever, you know, play with us?" And again Eva responds by acting as though this is a completely ridiculous question:

Play? Wasn't nobody playin' in 1895. Just 'cause you got it good now you think it was always this good? 1895 was a killer girl. Things was bad. Niggers was dying like flies...What would I look like leapin' 'round that little old room playin' with youngins with three beets to my name?

Eva's responses suggest that finding the means for material survival was not only the most important gesture of care, but that it precluded all other gestures. This is a way of thinking that many black people share. It makes care for material well-being synonymous with the practice of loving. The reality is, of course, that even in a context of material privilege, love may be absent. Concurrently, within the context of poverty, where one must struggle to make ends meet, one might keep a spirit of love alive by making a space for playful engagement, the expression of creativity, for individuals to receive care and attention in relation to their emotional well-being, a kind of care that attends to hearts and minds as well as stomachs. As contemporary black people commit ourselves to collective recovery, we must recognize that attending to our emotional well-being is just as important as taking care of our material needs.

It seems appropriate that this dialogue on love in *Sula* takes place between two black women, between mother and daughter, for their interchange symbolizes a legacy that will be passed on through the generations. In fact, Eva does not nurture Hannah's spiritual growth, and Hannah does not nurture the spiritual growth of her daughter, Sula. Yet, Eva does embody a certain model of "strong" black womanhood that is practically deified in black life. It is precisely her capacity to repress emotions and do whatever is needed for the continuation of material life that is depicted as the source of her strength. It is a kind of "instrumental" way of thinking about human needs, one that is echoed in the contemporary song Tina Turner sings—"What's love got to do with it?"

Living in a capitalist economy clearly informs the way black people think about love. In his essay, "Love and Need: Is Love a Package or a Message?" the Catholic monk Thomas Merton explains the way we are taught, via a market economy and the mass media that promotes it, to think of ourselves and of love as a commodity. His comments are worth quoting at length:

> Love is regarded as a deal. The deal presupposes that we all have needs which have to be fulfilled by means of exchange. In order to make a deal you have to appear in the market with a worthwhile product, or if the product is worthless, you can get by if you dress it up in a good-looking package. We unconsciously think of ourselves as objects for sale on the market...In doing this we come to consider ourselves and others not as *persons* but as *products*—as "goods," or in other words, as packages. We appraise one another commercially. We size each other up and make deals with a view to our own profit. We do not give ourselves in love, we make a deal that will enhance our own product, and therefore no deal is final.

Since so much of black life experience has been about the struggle to gain access to material goods, it makes sense that many of us not only over-value materiality but that we are also more vulnerable to the kind of thinking that commodifies feelings and makes it appear that they are only another kind of "material" need that can be satisfied within the same system of exchange used with other goods.

The combined forces of racist and sexist thinking have had a particularly negative influence on black women's attitudes about our relation to material goods. Not only have we been socialized to think of our bodies as a "product" to be exchanged, we are also made to feel that it is our responsibility to deliver needed products to others. Given that so many black women are the sole providers in black households, as Eva is in *Sula*, it is not surprising that we are often obsessed with material comfort, with finding the means to provide material well-being for ourselves and others. And, in this role, black women may be most unwilling to cultivate the practice of loving. We may be quite dedicated to caring for the needs of others, particularly material needs. Our need to love and be loved may be fundamentally denied, however. After all, it is ultimately "easier to worry about how you gonna' get a dollar to buy the latest product than it is to worry about whether there will be love in your house."

Love needs to be present in every black female's life, in all of our houses. It is the absence of love that has made it so difficult for us to stay alive or, if alive, to live fully. When we love ourselves we want to live fully. Whenever people talk about black women's lives, the emphasis is rarely on transforming society so that we can live fully, it is almost always about applauding how well we have "survived" despite harsh circumstances or how we can survive in the future. When we love ourselves, we know that we must do more than survive. We must have the means to live fully. To live fully, black women can no longer deny our need to know love.

If we would know love, we must first learn how to respond to inner emotional needs. This may mean undoing years of socialization where we have been taught that such needs are unimportant. Let me give an example. In her recently published book, *The Habit of Surviving: Black Women's Strategies for Life,* Kesho Scott opens the book sharing an incident from her life that she feels taught her important survival skills:

> Thirteen years tall, I stood in the living room doorway. My clothes were wet. My hair was mangled. I was in tears, in shock, and in need of my mother's warm arms. Slowly, she looked me up and down, stood up from the couch and walked towards me, her body clenched in criticism. Putting her hands on her hips and planting herself, her shadow falling over my face, she asked in a voice of barely suppressed rage, "What happened?" I flinched as if struck by the unexpected anger and answered, "They put my head in the toilet. They say I can't swim with them." "They" were eight white girls at my high school. I reached out to hold her, but she roughly brushed my hands aside and said, "Like hell! Get your coat. Let's go."

Straight-away it should be evident that Kesho was not learning that her emotional needs should be addressed at this moment. In her next sentences she asserts: "My mother taught me a powerful and enduring lesson that day. She taught me that I would have to fight back against racial and sexual injustice." Obviously, this is an important survival strategy for black women. But Kesho was also learning an unhealthy message at the same time. She was made to feel that she did not deserve comfort after a traumatic painful experience, that indeed she was "out-of-line" to even be seeking emotional solace, and that her individual needs were not as important as the collective struggle to resist racism and sexism. Imagine how different this story would read if we were told that as soon as Kesho walked into the room, obviously suffering distress, her mother had comforted her, helped repair the damage to her appearance, and then shared with her the necessity of confronting (maybe not just then, it would depend on her psychological state whether she could emotionally handle a confrontation) the racist white students who had assaulted her. Then Kesho would have known, at age thirteen, that her emotional well-being was just as important as the collective struggle to end racism and sexism— that indeed these two experiences are linked.

Many black females have learned to deny our inner needs while we develop our capacity to cope and confront in public life. This is why we can often appear to be functioning well on jobs but be utterly dysfunctional in private. You know what I am talking about. Undoubtedly you know a black woman who looks together, in control on the job, and when you drop by her house unexpectedly for a visit, aside from the living room, every other space looks like a tornado hit it, everything dirty and in disarray. I see this chaos and disorder as a reflection of the inner psyche, of the absence of well-being. Yet until black females believe, and hopefully learn when we are little girls, that our emotional well-being matters, we cannot attend to our needs. Often we replace recognition of inner emotional needs with the longing to control. When we deny our real needs, we tend to feel fragile, vulnerable, emotionally unstable, and untogether. Black females often work hard to cover up these conditions. And we cover up by controlling, by seeking to oversee or dominate everyone around us. The message we tell ourselves is, "I can't be falling apart because I have all this power over others."

Let us return to the mother in Kesho's story. What if the sight of her wounded and hurt daughter called to mind the mother's deep unaddressed inner wounds? What if she was critical, harsh, or just downright mean, because she did not want to break down, cry, and stop being the "strong black woman?" And yet, if she had cried, her daughter might have felt her pain was shared, that it was fine to name that you are in pain, that we do not have to keep the hurt bottled up inside us. What the mother did was what many of us have witnessed our mothers doing in similar circumstances—she took control. She was domineering, even her physical posture dominated. Clearly, this mother wanted her black female presence to have more "power" than that of the white girls.

A fictional model of black mothering that shows us a mother able to respond fully to her daughters when they are in pain is depicted in Ntozake Shange's novel *Sassafrass, Cypress and Indigo*. Throughout this novel, Shange's black female characters are strengthened in their capacity to self-actualize by a loving mother. Even though she does not always agree with their choices she respects them and offers them solace. Here is part of a letter she writes to Sassafrass who is "in trouble" and wants to come home. The letter begins with the exclamation: "Of course you can come home! What do you think you could do to yourself that I wouldn't love my girl?" First giving love and acceptance, Hilda later chastises, then expresses love again:

> You and Cypress like to drive me crazy with all this experimental living. You girls need to stop chasing the coon by his tail. And I know you know what I'm talking about...Mark my words. You just come on home and we'll straighten out whatever it is that's crooked in your thinking. There's lots to do to keep busy. And nobody around to talk foolish talk or experiment with. Something can't happen every day. You get up. You

**Living to Love**

eat, go to work, come back, eat again, enjoy some leisure, and go back to bed. Now, that's plenty for most folks. I keep asking myself where did I go wrong? Yet I know in my heart I'm not wrong. I'm right. The world's going crazy and trying to take my children with it. Okay. Now I'm through with all that. I love you very much. But you're getting to be a grown woman and I know that too. You come back to Charleston and find the rest of yourself. Love, Mama

It troubled me that it was difficult to find autobiographical narratives where black daughters describe loving interactions with black mothers. Overall, in fiction and autobiography, black mothers are more likely to be depicted as controlling, manipulative, and dominating, withholding love to maintain power over. If, as Jessica Benjamin suggests in *The Bonds of Love,* it is "mutual recognition" that disrupts the possibility of domination, then it is possible to speculate that black women who suffer a lack of recognition often feel the need to control others as a way to be noticed, to be seen as important. In Kesho's story the mother refuses to see her daughter's pain. By erasing her pain, she also erases that part of herself that hurts. And the message she gives is you can deny pain by the experience of power, in this case the power to return to a setting where you have been hurt and demand retribution. If black women were more loved and loving, the need to dominate others, particularly in the role of mother, would not be so intense. It is healing for black women who are obsessed with the need to control, to be "right," to practice letting go.

The great black civil rights activist Septima Clarke names that her personal growth was enhanced by letting go the need to be in control. For her this meant unlearning dependency on hierarchical models that suggest the person in power is always right. At one time she believed that whites always knew better than blacks what was good for our well-being. In *Ready from Within,* she declares:

> Because I had a very strong disciplined mother, who felt that whatever she had in her mind was right, I felt that whatever I had in my mind was right, too. I found out that I needed to change my way of thinking, and in changing my way of thinking I had to let people understand that their way of thinking was not the only way.

The art and practice of loving begins with our capacity to recognize and affirm ourselves. That is why so many self-help books encourage us to look at ourselves in the mirror and talk to the image we see there. Recently, I noticed that what I do with the image that I see in the mirror is very unloving. I inspect it. From the moment I get out of bed and look at myself in the mirror, I am evaluating. The point of the evaluation is not to provide self-affirmation but to critique. Now this was a common practice in our household. When the six of us girls made our way downstairs to the world inhabited by father, mother, and brother, we entered the world of "critique." We were looked over and told all that was wrong. Rarely did one hear a positive evaluation.

Replacing negative critique with positive recognition has made me feel more empowered as I go about my day. Affirming ourselves is the first step in the direction of cultivating the practice of being inwardly loving. I choose to use the phrase "inwardly loving" over self-love, because the very notion of "self" is so inextricably bound up with how we are seen by and in relation to others. Within a racist/sexist society, the larger culture will not socialize black women to know and acknowledge that our inner lives are important. Decolonized black women must name that reality in accord with others among us who understand as well that it is vital to nurture the inner life. As we examine our inner life, we get in touch with the world of emotions and feelings. Allowing ourselves to feel, we affirm our right in be inwardly loving. Once I know what I feel, I can also get in touch with those needs I can satisfy or name those needs that can only be satisfied in communion or contact with others.

Where is the love when a black woman looks at herself and says: "I see inside me somebody who is ugly, too dark, too fat, too afraid—somebody nobody would love, 'cause I don't even like what I see;" or maybe: "I see inside me somebody who is so hurt, who is just like a ball of pain and I don't want to look at her 'cause I can't do nothing about that pain." The love is absent. To make it present, the individual has to first choose to see herself, to just look at that inner self without blame or censure. And once she names what she sees, she might think about whether that inner self deserves or needs love.

I have never heard a black woman suggest during confessional moments in a support group that she does not need love. She may be in denial about that need but it doesn't take much self-interrogation to break through this denial. If you ask most black women straight-up if they need love—the answer is likely to be yes. To give love to our inner selves we must first give attention, recognition, and acceptance. Having let ourselves know that we will not be punished for acknowledging who we are or what we feel we can name the problems we see. I find it helpful to interview myself, and I encourage my sisters to do the same. Sometimes its hard for me to get immediately in touch with what I feel, but if I ask myself a question, an answer usually emerges.

Sometimes when we look at ourselves, and see our inner turmoil and pain, we do not know how to address it. That's when we need to seek help. I call loved ones sometimes and say, "I have these feelings that I don't understand or know how to address, can you help me?" There are many black females who cannot imagine asking for help, who see this as a sign of weakness. This is another negative debilitating worldview we should unlearn. It is a sign of personal power to be able to ask for help when you need it. And we find that asking for what we need when we need it is an experience that enhances rather than diminishes personal power. Try it and see. Often we wait until a crisis situation has happened when we are compelled by circumstance to seek the help of others. Yet, crisis can often be avoided if we seek help when we recognize that we are no longer able to function well in a given situation. For black women who are addicted to being controlling, asking for help can be a loving practice of surrender, reminding us that we do not always have to be in charge. Practicing being inwardly loving, we learn not only what our souls need but we begin to understand better the needs of everyone around us as well.

Black women who are *choosing* for the first time (note the emphasis on choosing) to practice the art and act of loving should devote time and energy showing love to other black people, both people we know and strangers. Within white-supremacist capitalist patriarchy, black people do not get enough love. And it's always exciting for those of us who are undergoing a process of decolonization to see other black people in our midst respond to loving care. Just the other day T., whom I mention in another chapter, told me that she makes a point of going into a local store and saying warm greetings to an older black man who works there. Recently, he wanted to know her name and then thanked her for the care that she gives to him. A few years ago when she was mired in self-hate, she would not have had the "will" to give him care. Now, she extends to him the level of care that she longs to receive from other black people when she is out in the world.

When I was growing up, I received "unconditional love" from black women who showed me by their actions that love did not have to be earned. They let me know that I deserved love; their care nurtured my spiritual growth. Black theologian and mystic Howard Thurman teaches us that we need to love one another without judging. Explaining this in an essay on Thurman's work, Walter Fluker writes:

> According to Thurman, there is within each individual a basic need to be cared for and understood in a relationship with another at a point that is beyond all that is good and evil. In religious experience, this inner necessity for love is fulfilled in encounter with God and in relation to others, the person is affirmed and becomes aware of being dealt with totally.

Many black people, and black women in particular, have become so accustomed to not being loved that we protect ourselves from having to acknowledge the pain such deprivation brings by acting like only white folks or other silly people sit around wanting to be loved. When I told a group of black women that I wanted there to be a world where I can feel love, feel myself giving and receiving love, every time I walk outside my house, they laughed.

For such a world to exist, racism and all other forms of domination would need to change. To the extent that I commit my life to working to end domination, I help transform the world so that it is that loving place that I want it to be.

Nikki Giovanni's "Woman Poem" has always meant a lot to me because it was one of the first pieces of writing that called out black women's self-hatred. Published in the anthology, *The Black Woman,* edited by Toni Bambara, this poem ends with the lines: "face me whose whole life is tied up to unhappiness cause it's the only for real thing i know." Giovanni not only names in this poem that black women are socialized to be caretakers, to deny our inner needs, she also names the extent to which self-hate can make us turn against those who are caring toward us. The black female narrator says: "how dare you care about me—you ain't got no good sense—cause i ain't shit you must be lower than that to care." This poem was written in 1968. Here we are, more than twenty years later, and black women are still struggling to break through denial to name the hurt in our lives and find ways to heal. Learning how to love is a way to heal. That learning cannot take place if we do not know what love is. Remember Stevie Wonder singing with tears in his eyes on national television: "I want to know what love is. I want you to show me."

I am empowered by the idea of love as the will to extend oneself to nurture one's own or another's spiritual growth because it affirms that love is an action, that it is akin to work. For black people it's an important definition because the focus is not on material well-being. And while we know that material needs must be met, collectively we need to focus our attention on emotional needs as well. There is that lovely biblical passage in "Proverbs" that reminds us: "Better a dinner of herbs, where love is, than a stalled ox and hatred therewith."

When we as black women experience fully the transformative power of love in our lives, we will bear witness publicly in a way that will fundamentally challenge existing social structures. We will be more fully empowered to address the genocide that daily takes the lives of black people—men, women, and children. When we know what love is, when we love, we are able to search our memories and see the past with new eyes; we are able to transform the present and dream the future. Such is love's power. Love heals.

# Chapter 10

# Sweet Communion

Though I've been writing this book sitting alone in a tiny study full of books, it has felt like a communal project. When I talk with black women friends, the Yams, and tell them, "It's finally happening—I'm doing the Yam book, you know the one on black female self-recovery," they say, "It's about time!"

Each step of the way during this writing I have been in ongoing conversations with black women who are passionate about recovery, with folks who feel they are struggling to find a healing place. In the midst of this writing, C., who had once been in a Sisters of the Yam support group (and who has been in a prolonged depression since a love affair ended), called in the late night frantically crying, saying: "This is it. I'm sitting here with fifty pills daring myself to take them, to get it over with. I'm just so tired." That sense of overwhelming loss and weariness that I hear in her voice is so familiar. It reminds me that there is a "world of hurt" inside us. It reminds me of a conversation I had with a black woman I met in the south months ago who held my hands tight and said again and again, "There's been so much hurt in me." Listening to C.

struggle with the longing to just give up, I think about the healing community that surrounds Velma in *The Salt Eaters* and I wonder if I can be that—a healing community.

I ask C., once a student in my black women's writers class, if she remembers reading *Sassafrass, Cypress and Indigo* and tell her that if it uplifted her spirits then she should read it again. But I mostly want to remind her of the recipes for healing, and give her my own made-on-the spot remedy for the easing of her pain. I tell her, "Get a pen. Stop crying so you can write this down and start working on it tonight." My remedy is long. But the last item on the list says: "When you wake up and find yourself living someplace where there is nobody you love and trust, no community, it is time to leave town—to pack up and go (you can even go tonight). And where you need to go is any place where there are arms that can hold you, that will not let you go."

We talk again, when she has come back to herself. Still I remind her of this last remedy. Then I tell her: "Girlfriend, I'm struggling with whether or not to write a chapter on relationships. I can't think of anything new to say. I don't wanna repeat all that stuff about black women and loneliness, and not having a man, cause every black woman don't even want a man, and do you have any thoughts on the subject?" Her contribution: "This man thing is not where it's at. And anyway, what's wrong with these dudes? And when are they gonna see that caring and being a friend is what's happening?" We talk and talk, agreeing that the *real deal* is learning to live and love in community. I share that, though I would like to have a committed relationship, I no longer believe that to be all that's necessary, and that I really want to build community. Remembering single black professional women in my childhood, who were all pretty much school teachers (some of whom had begun their careers at that historical moment when to make that choice was also to elect to remain unmarried since married women were not allowed to teach), I could not recall any of them lamenting their life-choices. Indeed, they were women of power leading fulfilled lives. And even though I know that they were lonely at times, that they did not have children they gave birth to, they were black women living in community. In profound ways, they were not alone. I have had the good fortune through my adult life to go "home" and talk with my teachers, those whose spirits guide and watch over me, and so my sense of their lives is not rooted in romantic fantasy.

Living in community, they found ways to cope with the gaps in their lives. It did not matter if they did not have children, for there was always some needy child in their midst upon whom they could shower love and care. They had their women's group, usually church related. And they had their romantic relationships, no doubt clandestine, but, of course, always known as everything in a small community is known. More than a year ago, my dearest friend from childhood days, decided to come live in the same town as I live in. We have nurtured and sustained our care for one another through long years. Just the other day we were talking about our lives, our hometown, and the black women we knew there whose lives did not fit the "norm." I asked Ehrai: "Do you think we will ever be able to know the kind of sweet long-lasting sense of community that they know? Do you think we can make it?" And with her usual wit, she answered: "There's always me, you, and Carre (her daughter), that's a start. You just need to find us a place."

Again and again, when I talk with black women who are engaged in a recovery and liberation process, whether they are in primary relationships or living as single parents or alone, I hear from all of us a concern about building a greater sense of community. It was maybe four years ago that I sat with Ntosake Shange and raised this question in relation to black women: "Where is the healing place?" That evening we had no answer. Now, I am more confident that community is a healing place. As black women come together with one another, with all the other folks in the world who are seeking recovery and liberation, we find the will to be well affirmed, we find ways to get what we need to ease the pain, to make the hurt go away. Some of us are more involved in structured recovery programs, in intense ongoing therapy, others of us do a lot of "home psychoanalysis" (my term for the therapy that friends, comrades and loved ones can do together daily). We are all discovering that the experience of community is crucial to wellness.

Much that is beautiful, magical, and unique in black culture has come from the experience of communal black life. Our communities have been truly undermined by addiction, whether they are rural or urban. Ironically, many of the drugs folks are addicted to, such as crack/cocaine, boost individualism and provide a false sense of agency and personal power. These drugs destroy the individual's capacity to experience community. When I first read Stanton Peele on addiction I was most struck by his insistence that addiction is not about relatedness, that helped me to begin to think about the way drug addiction has undermined black life by undermining our capacity to

build and sustain community. In *Love and Addiction,*
Peele offers the insight that "the antithesis of addiction is
a true relatedness to the world." By showing the ways our
notion of relationship, of love, promotes the development
of unhealthy dependencies, Peele calls attention to the
need to transform relations as we know them. To recon-
ceptualize our relational lives in terms of building community is a way to counter the addictive pattern. Peele
asserts:

> The interdependency of all individuals and organiza-
> tions makes the elimination of addiction contingent
> upon basic social change. But this same interdepend-
> ency means that if we work to influence those institu-
> tions that we normally deal with, we can make a
> contribution which will be felt throughout the entire
> system. In particular, the family is a place where any
> individual can be an immediate force for change.
> When we find new ways to relate to our parents, our
> mates, and our children—say, by making those rela-
> tionships less exclusive and obligatory—we have an
> impact on all aspects of our social structure. When
> individuals practice the art of loving in a context
> where they make various trusting relationships, we
> are less likely to reproduce the notion that it is "enough"
> to love just one person in a primary relationship.

One of the most harmful cultural myths that circu-
lates in our daily lives is the notion that we can leave
dysfunctional family settings and be ready to love when
we meet that "one" special person. By seeking to transform
and heal all our various relationships, we begin to create
a communal ethos where we learn how to experience
intimacy and how to love. In families where the notion of
domination reigns supreme, where exercising power and
control by any means necessary is the norm, there is little

hope that this will be a place where people can learn how to love. In *Lost in the Land of Oz,* Madonna Kolbenschlag suggests that the contemporary crisis in family life, the exposure to family violence, may generate the will to change. She, too, sees the development of community as necessary to promote and sustain change:

> Men and women cannot solve their problems of power, responsibility, and relationship alone. We are, whether as individuals, couples, or nuclear families, dwarfed by the task. We cannot evolve new roles and new familial arrangements without support, without a caring and intervening community, and most certainly not without a social order and social policy that promotes these ends...Honestly facing the abandonment and absence of a caring social environment, which is the real situation for most of us, can create the energy for imaginative restructuring of the shape of our lives. Hurt is hope's home—if we truly acknowledge that we are hurt and broken.

The focus on building community necessarily challenges a culture of domination that privileges individual well-being over collective effort.

The rise of narcissistic individualism among black people has undermined traditional emphasis on community. The culture of poverty that led to the development of a strong ethic of communalism among the black poor, an emphasis on sharing skills and resources, is swiftly eroding. In part, television plays a tremendous role in advancing both the cause of individualism and the identification of the poor with the values and ethos of the ruling class. When we consider, too, what the feminization of poverty means for black life, it is tragically evident that masses of black women are and will be struggling to make ends meet, to raise families with little or no material resources.

Given this situation, black women have a particular investment in bringing to our families, to black life in general, a renewed concern with making community.

Ironically, just when black people need to affirm the importance of community, when we need to redevelop an ethos that emphasizes collective well-being, we are witnessing a proliferation of the false assumption that somehow black life can be redeemed if we develop strong black patriarchies. This is certainly the reactionary message of Shahrazad Ali's *The Blackman's Guide to Understanding the Blackwoman.* All our observations of patriarchal white families in the United States should indicate that reproducing this unhealthy model in black face would do little to heal the woundedness and brokenness in black life. While it is important that we call attention to the particular ways black men are assaulted, brutalized, dehumanized, and slaughtered in this society, we must simultaneously acknowledge how much of this violence is promoted by patriarchal thinking. Hence, it cannot be meaningfully addressed by black people promoting patriarchy.

Recently, appearing on a television talk show focusing on black family life, I was stunned to hear a young black male filmmaker (who has made a film in which the downtrodden black patriarchal husband brutally murders his wife) and a black male congressperson insist that black men do not need mental health care; "They need jobs, they need spending money to have self-esteem." Intervening, I suggested that it is no longer useful for black people struggling to survive and recover ourselves to think in either/or terms. Yes! Black men need jobs, but being employed will not automatically mean that they will use the money they earn to take care of families (there are many employed male patriarchs of all races who do not provide for families) or enhance self-esteem. Yet, there is a dignity to be found in work and in being able to provide for one's material needs. We still have to keep in mind though that there are many men, and many black men, who make lots of money but have low self-esteem, who are violent in domestic life.

Breaking with traditional patriarchal thinking, and the negative masculine identity it promotes, would enable black men to take seriously their mental health and well-being. If black people disinvest from the patriarchal notion that "real" men do not need to address their emotional life and their psychic well-being, we can begin to create strategies for social change that will enhance black male life and as a consequence all our lives. As more black men become critical of sexism and seek to reconstruct masculinity, we will see a change in the quality of black male life. One of the tragic implications of black communities' embracing Ali's work is its promotion of the kind of patriarchal thinking that holds black women responsible for the well-being of black men. Black male writer and publisher Haki Madhubuti correctly identifies this book as a "never-ending guide for non-functional relationships." He states further: "It is a call to return to the unquestioned, uncritical patriarch, the return of the mythic Black king. This is a call to put and keep Black women in their 'place' as defined by Black men." Yet many black women who have internalized sexist thinking are attempting to adapt their behavior to the model set forth in Ali's book.

In no way breaking from white, patriarchal norms, *The Blackman's Guide to Understanding the Blackwoman* extols the virtues of the dominated submissive female. Black women who feel "guilty" about the hurt and woundedness of black men in this society are vulnerable to the kind of thinking that suggests we are not only responsible for this hurt but able to make life better by being submissive. Sadly, this assumption intensifies our problems since it is an unrealistic assessment of all the factors that contribute to pain in black life, in black men in particular. Collective black self-recovery, and the self-recovery of black women in particular, must have a feminist dimension if black women want to accurately name the factors, the forces of domination, that undermine black life. Until masses of black women understand what sexism is and how it leads to the denigration and devaluation of black womanhood and black life, there will be no collective understanding of the ways in which life-threatening patriarchy, misogyny, and male domination are destructive forces in our lives that must be challenged and changed.

There is no black woman I know who is engaged in a process of self-recovery who is not also involved with rethinking the sexist attitudes towards women that are the norm in this society. Though many of these women do not call themselves "feminist," they are using feminist thinking to inspire and affirm changes that they are making in their personal lives. Watching Spike Lee's film *Mo' Better Blues,* black women of all ages were disturbed by the portrait of black heterosexuality this film promotes. Lee presents a conventional image of the dominating black female and the creative black man who is beaten down both by her and society. Even though the black male "hero" ultimately comes to a black woman, pleading with her to "save his life," this vision is so limited as to offer us no possibility for redemptive change. Black women have tried for years to save the lives of black men. We have stayed in destructive relationships trying to hold it all together. And one of the most meaningful lessons self-recovery teaches us is that it is the individual's acceptance of responsibility for changing, for "saving" his or her own life, that leads to transformation. That is why no matter how great the healing powers are of the black female elders in *The Salt Eaters,* they can heal Velma only if she wants to be well.

When black men work against the racist/sexist thinking that socializes them to devalue their own lives, and choose to work for self-recovery, black women can affirm this process without being seduced into unproductive co-dependent relationships. Since healthy black women do not see ourselves in competition with black men, we want to share with them the joy of recovery and look forward to those moments of mutual recovery. Significantly, gay black men are at the forefront of black male groups who are most concerned with rethinking masculinity, with letting go of old sexist paradigms and changing the way they relate to black women and one another.

When we think of collective black self-recovery in communal terms, we have a paradigm for well-being that does not reproduce the heterosexism that is the norm in this culture. Working to end homophobia, in fact, is central to our self-recovery. In authentic life-sustaining black communities, there is a place for all of us in our diversity of sexual needs, desires, practices, and commitments. Traditional black communities, though homophobic, did not deny or hide the contribution of black gay people. The current movie *A Rage in Harlem* depicts a meaningful bond between a black straight man and a gay man, showing that their sense of community and kinship is life-sustaining. This portrayal reminds us of the ways in which traditional black communities were not invested in the politics of inclusion and exclusion that has become more the norm now as we have assimilated the dominant culture's notions of what is appropriate. In both her nonfiction writing and her fiction, Toni Morrison has consistently worked to create awareness that such communities existed, that they were characterized by the way "difference" was welcomed and accepted, by an openness and generosity of spirit that was the underlying value system shaping human relations. We can learn progressive models of social organization by studying the past, by looking at these black communities.

Despite an emphasis on racial uplift and black pride, these communities did not engage a narrow nationalism rooted in the politics of domination and exclusion. White people, and any "others," who wanted to find a place in those communities were not rejected. They were taught instead how to live with and among black people in the spirit of true community. These traditional black communities are similar to what Buddhist monk Thich Nhat Hanh calls "communities of resistance." They were places where black people could retain our sense of wholeness and integrity. Nhat Hanh teaches that "communities of resistance should be places where people can return to themselves more easily, where the conditions are such that they can heal themselves and recover their wholeness." Black people are desperately in need of such communities today.

Historically, black women were fully engaged in constructing communities of resistance. The sexist thinking of black men may have inhabited their involvement but it did not make them quit or give up. Contemporary black females seeking self-recovery can renew our commitment to building communities of resistance, by carrying on this legacy. That practice can start in our homes. Thich Nhat Hanh says that the purpose of resistance is "to seek the healing of yourself in order to be able to see clearly." He helps us to understand that the environments we live in determine and influence our ability to heal:

> A pagoda, a temple, a church, is built in a way that when you enter you recover yourself; you come into contact with the absolute reality, with God, with Buddha, with Buddhahood. And that is why the recovering of self is seen in architecture, in decorative art, in sacred music, in many things like that. So that when you come to the church or the temple you are helped by these things to return to yourself. I think our communities of resistance should be built like a church or a temple where everything you see expresses the tendency to be oneself, to go back to oneself, to come into communion with reality.

In black life our homes can be such places, irrespective of our class status. We do not need lots of money to create environments that are, to use Nhat Hanh's words, "beautiful, healing, refreshing both in surroundings and in substance."

In many of the preceding chapters, I have called attention to the way our sense of community is deepened when we love ourselves and one another. Often black women are very judgmental of one another. We understand that this practice of harsh critique has cultural roots yet it breeds discord and discontent among us. Unlearning the need to judge others mean-spiritedly is crucial if we are to make beloved communities and healing places. Thich Nhat Hanh makes this contribution to our thinking about building community: "Do not judge each other too easily, too quickly, in terms of ideology, of point of view, strategies, things like that. Try to see the real person, the one with whom you live. You might discover aspects that will enrich you. It's like a tree that can shelter you." Working together to build communities that foster a sense of kinship that goes beyond blood ties or bonds of friendship, black women expand our horizons. When communities of resistance are everywhere the norm in our lives, we will not be without a circle of love or a healing place.

Such communities of resistance can emerge around our struggles for personal self-recovery as well as our efforts to organize collectively to bring about social change. We grow closer in struggle. The civil rights movement is a grand example of the way working to transform society can sweeten and strengthen community bonds. While I have emphasized the importance of working for self-actualization in the individual's life, we learn about ourselves and test our values in active practice with others. Choosing to be self-actualized and then working to build communities of resistance that are particularly focused on social and political concerns is always necessary.

Organizations like The Black Women's Health Project that begin with small groups of black women coming together and then expand to national organizations show the power of our coming together to serve one another collectively. Small presses like Kitchen Table Press are another example of the ways we move our individual quest for self-recovery into a larger arena. Significantly, we can begin this process wherever we are. The Sisters of the Yam support groups began in my office, then in dormitories, and finally in homes. While we focused on personal concerns, we linked those concerns to institutional issues and connected the two. No level of individual self-actualization alone can sustain the marginalized and oppressed. We must be linked to collective struggle, to communities of resistance that move us outward, into the world.

Chapter 11

# The Joy of Reconciliation

*Over the years I have worried about losing not only my mother and other members of my family, but also poets, singers, philosophers, prophets, political activists. And many of these we have all lost, sometimes to sickness, accident or disease; sometimes to assassination. But I have found that where there is spiritual union with other people, the love one feels for them keeps the circle unbroken and the bonds between us and them strong, whether they are dead or alive. Perhaps that is one of the manifestations of heaven on earth.*

—Alice Walker, *Living by the Word*

Healing inner wounds makes reconciliation possible. Reconciliation is one of my favorite words. Evoking our capacity to restore to harmony that which has been broken, severed, and disrupted. The very word serves as a constant reminder in my life that we can come together with those who have hurt us, with those whom we have caused pain, and experience sweet communion.

To be at peace, black women, especially those among us who have been deeply wounded and hurt, must release the bitterness we hold within us. Bitterness is like a poison. When it's inside us, it spreads even to the parts of the self that allow us to feel joy and a spirit of celebration. Yet many of us choose to hold onto pain through the cultivation of bitterness and an unforgiving heart. Holding onto pain with bitterness may also be a way we hold on to our attachment to individuals who should no longer control our lives but continue to do so because our bitterness lets them. For example, black women in long-time marriages with men who psychologically abuse them often become obsessed with remaining at the center of this negative drama. Bitterness and hatred keep their negative connection to their partners alive, keep the drama happening. Even though it is wounding, each party clings to these feelings. When we remain unreconciled with those who have hurt us, it is usually a sign that we have not fully reconciled with ourselves. When we give ourselves love and peace, we can give these gifts to others. It's really impossible to live a life in love while hoping that harm and hurt will come to others.

Throughout our history in the United States, black people have suffered so much, and yet collectively, at those historical moments when our suffering was most intense, we practiced the art of compassion and forgiveness. It seems that back then, wise black elders knew that our inner peace, our capacity to know joy as a people, was intimately linked to our ability to let go of bitterness, to forgive. Black southern midwife Onnie Lee Logan's oral autobiography *Motherwit* shares this wisdom throughout its pages as she describes dedicating her life to bringing black and white children safely into the world. Sharing memories passed down in her family history of the pain slavery caused (Miss Onnie was born in the early 1900s), she names those sorrows while evoking the need for black people to let go bitterness:

> Out of all that we went along like happy-go-lucky. No ill will in our heart or mind or nothin. We lived like human bein's supposed to live. That hasn't made me resentful at all. I'm glad God kep' me. I'm so happy I don't know what else I'd want to do. You know why? It's paying off. Indeed white people have done black people wrong. And you know what: The general run of em know it. They admit it. A lot of em that won't admit it knows it. But there's a plenty of em that admit it. God did not let it deal with me too much and I's glad cause if you get yo' mind set on that you cain't go on to nothin else.

This passage makes clear that Miss Onnie did not see the need to forgive or be compassionate as synonymous with ceasing to hold people accountable for wrongdoing. In their historical role as caretakers, black women practiced the art of compassion and knew that forgiveness not only eased the pain of the heart but made love possible.

This powerful legacy, handed down by generations of caring black women, was undermined by contemporary black liberation struggles that devalued these women's legacy. The inability of the sixties' struggle for black liberation to fundamentally transform this society by ending racism created a lot of despair in the minds and hearts of black people. Many of us ceased to hope that a real change would ever come. And there was a great welling up of bitterness and hatred toward white people (conservative and liberal alike) who showed themselves unwilling to divest of white supremacy and fully resist racism. That bitterness has lingered in the collective psyche of black people and poisons our relationships with one another.

Compelled by the desire to forge militant struggle against racist domination, many black people felt we had to discard the idea that it was important to love one's enemies, to forgive. These values came to be seen by many as signs of weakness. Such thinking was fundamentally misguided. In his powerful sermon opposing the Vietnam War, "A Time to Break Silence," Martin Luther King reminded us that we needed a "genuine revolution of values" that would enable everyone to militantly oppose oppression here and globally without forsaking our capacity to love. Calling for the development of a universal loyalty to world community, King spoke of love as a revolutionary, empowering force:

> This call for a world-wide fellowship that lifts neighborly concern beyond one's tribe, race, class and nation is in reality a call for an all-embracing and unconditional love for all men. This oft misunderstood and misinterpreted concept—so readily dismissed by the Nietzsches of the world as a weak and cowardly force—has now become an absolute necessity for the survival of man. When I speak of love I am not speaking of some sentimental and weak response. I am speaking of that force which all of the great religions have seen as the supreme unifying principle of life. Love is somehow the key that unlocks the door which leads to ultimate reality. This Hindu-Moslem-Christian-Jewish-Buddhist belief about ultimate reality is beautifully summed up in the first epistle of Saint John: "Let us love one another; for love is God and everyone that loveth is born of God and knoweth God. He that loveth not knoweth not God; for God is love. If we love one another God dwelleth in us, and his love is perfected in us."

It was uplifting to black people's Spirit to cultivate love. And by so doing we nurtured our capacity to forgive, to be compassionate. Shutting the doors of the self that could be compassionate toward white people meant that we also shut the doors that would enable us to show compassion to one another.

Compassion is rooted in understanding. When I critically examine my parents' lives, all that they suffered and endured, the many ways they did not receive the tender loving care that should have been their birthright, I cannot maintain anger or bitterness towards them. I understand them and the forces that made them who they are. And this understanding enables me to feel compassion, to let go of all willingness to blame. Our capacity to forgive always allows us to be in touch with our own agency (that is the power to act on our own behalf to change a situation). Enslaved black people clearly understood the need to remain in touch with all those aspects of the self that enabled them to experience agency. Without agency we collapse into passivity, inertia, depression, and despair.

In *Peace, Love and Healing,* Bernie Siegel makes the point that "people may learn helplessness if they have had repeated experiences of being unable to change external circumstances through their own efforts" resulting in their feeling "a kind of fatalism that will be applied to all the events that befall them in a lifetime." I believe that now more than ever before in our history black people are victimized by learned helplessness, that renewing our collective capacity to know compassion, to forgive, would be healing to our spirit, restoring to many of us a lost sense of agency.

When black women recover fully and exercise our will to be compassionate, to forgive, this will have a healing impact on black life. The sexism of the sixties' black power movement devalued the necessary life-sustaining contributions black women had made to liberation struggle, and this generated not only a lot of despair in black women but unexpressed rage. There are many black women who hold within them intense anger toward black men for not making life better for them. Certainly, these are the women who most internalize sexist assumptions that it is the male responsibility to maintain life, to provide. In reality, that responsibility is mutual and must be shared.

As black women collectively act compassionately toward ourselves, we will be able to extend a more loving compassion to black men as well. This compassion will be rooted in understanding all that black men experience and will not be the kind of negative sympathy that is expressed when black women act as though we somehow need to "pity" black men because "they just can't deliver." Were all black people to collectively release the feelings of bitterness we hold towards one another, there would be a great renewal of spiritual strength.

Compassion and forgiveness make reconciliation possible. Compassion combines the capacity to empathize with another's distress and the will and desire to ease that distress. As black women learn how to ease the distress we feel, our ability to generously give to others (not as self-sacrificing martyrs) will be strengthened. We will then have no need to control and bind others to us by always reminding them about what we have done on their behalf. Rather than seeing giving care as diminishing us, we will experience the kind of caregiving that enriches the giver. When we feel like martyrs, we cannot develop compassion. For compassion requires that we be able to stand outside ourselves and identify with someone else. It is fundamentally rooted in the ability to empathize.

My understanding of the way of compassion has been deepened by the teachings of Vietnamese Buddhist monk and peace activist Thich Nhat Hanh. In *Peace Is Every Step,* he teaches about "understanding" by sharing the story of a brother who goes to wake his sister one morning. She responds with hostility. Before her brother can retaliate in kind:

> He remembers that during the night his sister coughed a lot, and he realizes that she must be sick. Maybe she behaved so meanly because she has a cold. At that moment, he understands, and he is not angry at all anymore. When you understand, you cannot help but love. You cannot get angry. To develop understanding, you have to practice looking at all living beings with the eyes of compassion. When you understand, you cannot help but love. And when you love, you naturally act in a way that can relieve the suffering of people.

Judging others, presuming to know why they are doing what they are doing, blocks our capacity to know compassion. Often black women judge each other harshly. Cultivating our capacity to empathize would deepen our bonds with one another.

Often we do not realize that the black woman we see as competing with us or treating us with disregard may be in need of sisterly care and recognition. If we cannot look past the surface and see what lies underneath we will not be able to give to one another the compassionate understanding we also need in our daily lives. It's important for us to remember that even the most trivial gesture can have a meaningful transformative impact in someone's life. I gave a talk recently and, though there were many people pouring in, a lone black woman caught my eye. When she found her seat, I went over to greet her. Weeks later I received a note from her. In it she wrote: "I was stunned by the spontaneous lovingness of a gesture you made towards me. It will take some time before I fully internalize the lessons of relatedness and sisterhood it showed me." Sisters, we need to ask ourselves how do we greet and meet one another in daily life, if it seems strange, odd, out-of-the ordinary to show one another regard and recognition.

Significantly, we are often competing with one another, with other black women we do not even know. The roots of this competition are again related to most black women's feelings that we are invisible. And that when visible we are competing for the "only one black woman allowed recognition here" slot constructed by racism and sexism. To resist this socialization, we need to cultivate compassion that is rooted in vigilant awareness of the positive life-affirming impact our presence can have on one another. Since we know that we are wounded, since we know in our hearts that racism and sexism hurt, that many of us are walking around surrounded by a wall to keep anymore pain from coming in, then this knowledge should create awareness, and this awareness should deepen our compassion.

If black women look at the world from a conventional negative perspective that would have us all believe there is only this little bit of anything good to go around and we must fight to get our part, then we can't really love one another. Black women who see the world as one big system of diminishing returns can only feel a constant fear that

someone else's gain means that they will suffer deprivation. This way of thinking mirrors the overall rise in
cultural narcissism and narrow notions of individualism
that are life-threatening to black people because we need
an ethic of communalism to live with dignity and integrity.
And black women must be willing to take a major role in
communicating this fact to the world. Concurrently, in our
roles as mothers, or as "pretend" mothers (people like me
who do not have blood children but who joyously adopt and
parent here and there), we can do so much to transform
the violence and pain in black life by giving peace and
understanding, by showing compassion.

Just yesterday I spoke with a working mother who
was expressing concern about the "hatefulness" that she
hears in her children's voices when they talk to one another. I suggested that she talk openly and honestly with
them about why it is important for black people to be good
to one another, about the bonds of love that make us a
family. I urged her to tape their conversations so that they
can hear how they speak to one another and interpret
what it means to them. Once that was done, I thought, she
could figure out and create rewards with them for a change
in behavior.

Individually, when we practice forgiveness in our
lives we cleanse our spirit of negative clutter and leave our
souls free. As Arnold and Barry Fox suggest in *Wake Up!
You're Alive:*

> Forgiveness is a glorious feeling that sets you free. But
> even if you already have the feeling of forgiveness
> inside of you, you must still say the words "I forgive
> you" out loud. That is vital. The words are in a sense
> an affirmation with a hidden meaning…Forgiveness
> instructs your subconscious to banish negative feel-

ings from your mind. When you say, "I forgive you" to someone you are also saying, "I want to be healthy" to yourself.

Genuine desire to change our world by cultivating compassion and the will to forgive should make us more able to vigilantly resist oppression and exploitation, to joyfully engage in oppositional struggle. I know that there are those among us who worry that being too forgiving will somehow diminish our ability to sustain resistance. Again, I think it important that we remember that forgiveness does not mean that we cease to assertively identify wrongs, hold others to account, and demand justice. It is because we can practice "forgiveness" and be transformed that we have the compassion and insight to see that the same is true for those who might appear to be "enemies." This is the true realization of justice—that we want what is peaceful and life-sustaining for all and not just for ourselves.

In my own life, I do "forgiveness" meditations. Sitting quietly in a peaceful location where I will not be disturbed, I visualize the image of individuals who I feel have hurt or injured me and I talk to them about what happened, how I feel, and express forgiveness. Yet, whenever we can, it is also important to express forgiveness directly, through the mail, over the phone, or in face-to-face conversation. Most of us who have been abused know that it is a healing moment when you are able to name to that person that you forgive them or, if they seek forgiveness, you respond with regard and compassion. Sometime this generous act makes reconciliation possible. Often when folks wrong us, they engage in self-punishment by no longer allowing themselves to experience our love and care. They may feel unworthy of our kindness. Forgiveness enables the restoration of mutual harmony. We can both start over again on an equal footing, no longer separated by whatever wrong occurred.

When I was growing up, my parents were not the only family members who hurt and wounded me, my siblings also persecuted me. More than ten years ago, one of my sisters, whom I was never close to, came to visit me. And I was so happy that we were having this reunion, this opportunity to get to know one another, I did not want to talk about the past. She felt a strong need to speak about the past and to ask forgiveness for the hurt she had caused me in childhood. The sweetness of her actions was revealed not only in the confirmation that what I remembered had really happened, but in the way it freed us to start anew. Today, she is a true friend and comrade in my life. And yet I know that we would not be in this marvelous sisterly bonding had she not had the courage to ask forgiveness and if I had not had the will to forgive. She was able to truly see that there was no bitterness in my heart about the past.

We have to forgive with our whole hearts. If we forgive in words but continue to harbor secret resentment, nothing really changes. When forgiveness happens, when there is compassion, the groundwork for reconciliation is possible. For me that is the ultimate joy: That we learn that there are no broken bonds that cannot be mended, no pain that cannot be assuaged.

# Chapter 12

# Touching the Earth

*I wish to live because life has within it that which is good, that which is beautiful, and that which is love. Therefore, since I have known all these things, I have found them to be reason enough and—I wish to live. Moreover, because this is so, I wish others to live for generations and generations and generations and generations.*

—Lorraine Hansberry, *To Be Young, Gifted, and Black*

When we love the earth, we are able to love ourselves more fully. I believe this. The ancestors taught me it was so. As a child I loved playing in dirt, in that rich Kentucky soil, that was a source of life. Before I understood anything about the pain and exploitation of the southern system of sharecropping, I understood that grown-up black folks loved the land. I could stand with my grandfather Daddy Jerry and look out at fields of growing vegetables, tomatoes, corn, collards, and know that this was his handiwork. I could see the look of pride on his face as I expressed wonder and awe at the magic of growing things. I knew that my grandmother Baba's backyard garden would yield beans, sweet potatoes, cabbage, and yellow squash, that she too would walk with pride among the rows and rows of growing vegetables showing us what the earth will give when tended lovingly.

From the moment of their first meeting, Native American and African people shared with one another a respect for the life-giving forces of nature, of the earth. African settlers in Florida taught the Creek Nation runaways, the "Seminoles," methods for rice cultivation. Native peoples taught recently arrived black folks all about the many uses of corn. (The hotwater cornbread we grew up eating came to our black southern diet from the world of the Indian.) Sharing the reverence for the earth, black and red people helped one another remember that, despite the white man's ways, the land belonged to everyone. Listen to these words attributed to Chief Seattle in 1854:

> How can you buy or sell the sky, the warmth of the land? The idea is strange to us. If we do not own the freshness of the air and the sparkle of the water, how can you buy them? Every part of this earth is sacred to my people. Every shining pine needle, every sandy shore, every mist in the dark woods, every clearing and humming insect is holy in the memory and experience of my people...We are part of the earth and it is part of us. The perfumed flowers are our sisters; the deer, the horse, the great eagle, these are our brothers. The rocky crests, the juices in the meadows, the body heat of the pony, and man—all belong to the same family.

The sense of union and harmony with nature expressed here is echoed in testimony by black people who found that even though life in the new world was "harsh, harsh," in relationship to the earth one could be at peace. In the oral autobiography of granny midwife Onnie Lee Logan, who lived all her life in Alabama, she talks about

the richness of farm life—growing vegetables, raising
chickens, and smoking meat. She reports:

> We lived a happy, comfortable life to be right outa
> slavery times. I didn't know nothin else but the farm
> so it was happy and we was happy...We couldn't do
> anything else but be happy. We accept the days as
> they come and as they were. Day by day until you
> couldn't say there was any great hard time. We over-
> looked it. We didn't think nothin about it. We just
> went along. We had what it takes to make a good livin
> and go about it.

Living in modern society, without a sense of history, it
has been easy for folks to forget that black people were
first and foremost a people of the land, farmers. It is easy
for folks to forget that at the first part of the 20th
century, the vast majority of black folks in the United
States lived in the agrarian south.

Living close to nature, black folks were able to cultivate a spirit of wonder and reverence for life. Growing food
to sustain life and flowers to please the soul, they were
able to make a connection with the earth that was ongoing
and life-affirming. They were witnesses to beauty. In
Wendell Berry's important discussion of the relationship
between agriculture and human spiritual well-being, *The
Unsettling of America,* he reminds us that working the
land provides a location where folks can experience a
sense of personal power and well-being:

> We are working well when we use ourselves as the
> fellow creature of the plants, animals, material, and
> other people we are working with. Such work is uni-
> fying, healing. It brings us home from pride and despair,
> and places us responsibly within the human estate. It
> defines us as we are: not too good to work without our

bodies, but too good to work poorly or joylessly or selfishly or alone.

There has been little or no work done on the psychological impact of the "great migration" of black people from the agrarian south to the industrialized north. Toni Morrison's novel *The Bluest Eye* attempts to fictively document the way moving from the agrarian south to the industrialized north wounded the psyches of black folk. Estranged from a natural world, where there was time for silence and contemplation, one of the "displaced" black folks in Morrison's novel, Miss Pauline, loses her capacity to experience the sensual world around her when she leaves southern soil to live in a northern city. The south is associated in her mind with a world of sensual beauty most deeply expressed in the world of nature. Indeed, when she falls in love for the first time she can name that experience only by evoking images from nature, from an agrarian world and near wilderness of natural splendor:

> When I first seed Cholly, I want you to know it was like all the bits of color from that time down home when all us chil'ren went berry picking after a funeral and I put some in the pocket of my Sunday dress, and they mashed up and stained my hips. My whole dress was messed with purple, and it never did wash out. Not the dress nor me. I could feel that purple deep inside me. And that lemonade Mama used to make when Pap came in out of the fields. It be cool and yellowish, with seeds floating near the bottom. And that streak of green them june bugs made on the tress that night we left from down home. All of them colors was in me. Just sitting there.

Certainly, it must have been a profound blow to the collective psyche of black people to find themselves struggling to make a living in the industrial north away from the land. Industrial capitalism was not simply changing the nature of black work life, it altered the communal practices that were so central to survival in the agrarian south. And it fundamentally altered black people's relationship to the body. It is the loss of any capacity to appreciate her body, despite its flaws, Miss Pauline suffers when she moves north.

The motivation for black folks to leave the south and move north was both material and psychological. Black folks wanted to be free of the overt racial harassment that was a constant in southern life and they wanted access to material goods—to a level of material well-being that was not available in the agrarian south where white folks limited access to the spheres of economic power. Of course, they found that life in the north had its own perverse hardships, that racism was just as virulent there, that it was much harder for black people to become landowners. Without the space to grow food, to commune with nature, or to mediate the starkness of poverty with the splendor of nature, black people experienced profound depression. Working in conditions where the body was regarded solely as a tool (as in slavery), a profound estrangement occurred between mind and body. The way the body was represented became more important than the body itself. It did not matter if the body was well, only that it appeared well.

Estrangement from nature and engagement in mind/body splits made it all the more possible for black people to internalize white-supremacist assumptions about black identity. Learning contempt for blackness, southerners transplanted in the north suffered both culture shock and soul loss. Contrasting the harshness of city

life with an agrarian world, the poet Waring Cuney wrote
this popular poem in the 1920s, testifying to lost connection:

> She does not know her beauty
> She thinks her brown body
> has no glory.
> If she could dance naked,
> Under palm trees
> And see her image in the river
> She would know.
> But there are no palm trees on the street,
> And dishwater gives back no images.

For many years, and even now, generations of black
folks who migrated north to escape life in the south,
returned down home in search of a spiritual nourishment,
a healing, that was fundamentally connected to reaffirm-
ing one's connection to nature, to a contemplative life
where one could take time, sit on the porch, walk, fish, and
catch lightning bugs. If we think of urban life as a location
where black folks learned to accept a mind/body split that
made it possible to abuse the body, we can better understand the growth of nihilism and despair in the black
psyche. And we can know that when we talk about healing
that psyche we must also speak about restoring our connection to the natural world.

Wherever black folks live we can restore our relationship to the natural world by taking the time to commune
with nature, to appreciate the other creatures who share
this planet with humans. Even in my small New York City
apartment I can pause to listen to birds sing, find a tree
and watch it. We can grow plants—herbs, flowers, vegetables. Those novels by African-American writers (women
and men) that talk about black migration from the agrar-

ian south to the industrialized north describe in detail the way folks created space to grow flowers and vegetables. Although I come from country people with serious green thumbs, I have always felt that I could not garden. In the past few years, I have found that I can do it—that many gardens will grow, that I feel connected to my ancestors when I can put a meal on the table of food I grew. I especially love to plant collard greens. They are hardy, and easy to grow.

In modern society, there is also a tendency to see no correlation between the struggle for collective black self-recovery and ecological movements that seek to restore balance to the planet by changing our relationship to nature and to natural resources. Unmindful of our history of living harmoniously on the land, many contemporary black folks see no value in supporting ecological movements, or see ecology and the struggle to end racism as competing concerns. Recalling the legacy of our ancestors who knew that the way we regard land and nature will determine the level of our self-regard, black people must reclaim a spiritual legacy where we connect our well-being to the well-being of the earth. This is a necessary dimension of healing. As Berry reminds us:

> Only by restoring the broken connections can we be healed. Connection is health. And what our society does its best to disguise from us is how ordinary, how commonly attainable, health is. We lose our health— and create profitable diseases and dependencies—by failing to see the direct connections between living and eating, eating and working, working and loving. In gardening, for instance, one works with the body to feed the body. The work, if it is knowledgeable, makes for excellent food. And it makes one hungry. The work thus makes eating both nourishing and joyful, not

consumptive, and keeps the eater from getting fat and weak. This health, wholeness, is a source of delight.

Collective black self-recovery takes place when we begin to renew our relationship to the earth, when we remember the way of our ancestors. When the earth is sacred to us, our bodies can also be sacred to us.

Chapter 13

# Walking in the Spirit

Writing was always a sanctuary for me in my wounded childhood, a place of confession, where nothing had to be hidden or kept secret. It has always been one of the healing places in my life. At the end of William Goyen's essay "Recovering," he states, "It is clear that writing—recovering life—for me is a spiritual task." Like Goyen, I believe that writing is "the work of the spirit." Lately, when I am asked to talk about what has sustained me in my struggle for self-recovery, I have been more willing to talk openly about a life lived in the spirit than in the past. In part, I have responded to the urgency and need I have witnessed in younger black females who speak with grave uncertainty and fear as they ponder whether or not they will be able to survive life's difficulties. And I have wanted to tell them the truth, that I am sustained by spiritual life, by my belief in divine spirits, what other folks often call "higher powers."

Spirituality sustains most black women I know who are engaged in recovery processes. For some of us, spiritual life is linked to traditional Christian faith. Others of us expand our horizons as we seek to give expression to our faith in gods, goddesses, or in higher powers. In *Feel the Fear and Do It Anyway,* Susan Jeffers acknowledges that many nonreligious folks are uncomfortable with the idea of the spiritual. Describing in a clear manner what is meant by this term, she explains, "When I speak of the spiritual, I speak of the Higher Self, the place within that is loving, kind, abundant, joyful..." Throughout our history in this country, black women have relied on spirituality to sustain us, to renew our hope, to strengthen our faith. This spirituality has often had a narrow dimension wherein we have internalized without question dogmatic views of religious life informed by intense participation in patriarchal religious institutions. My purpose here is not to critique more conventional expressions of religious life. Indeed, the spiritual and the religious are not necessarily one and the same. My intent is to share the insight that cultivating spiritual life can enhance the self-recovery process and enable the healing of wounds. Jeffers suggests:

> Too many of us seem to be searching for something "out there" to make our lives complete. We feel alienated, lonely and empty. No matter what a we do or have, we never feel fulfilled. This feeling of emptiness or intense loneliness is our clue that we are off course, and that we need to correct our direction. Often we think that the correction lies in a new mate, house, car, job, or whatever. Not so. I believe what all of us are really searching for is this divine essence within ourselves.

In fiction by contemporary black women writers, healing takes place only when black female characters find the divine spirit within and nurture it. This is true for Avey in *Praisesong for the Widow,* for Celie in *The Color Purple,* for Baby Suggs in *Beloved,* for Indigo in *Sassa-*

*frass, Cypress and Indigo,* and countless other characters. For some of these characters, spirituality is linked to Christian faith, for others, African and Caribbean religous traditions. And in some cases, like that of Shug in *The Color Purple,* a break must occur with Christianity in order for a new spirituality to emerge. Jeffers suggests that unless we "consciously or unconsciously tap that spiritual part within" ourselves, "we will experience perpetual discontent." This same message is conveyed in black women's fiction. However, black women seeking healing want to know how we can actualize divine essence in our everyday lives.

Living a life in the spirit, a life where our habits of being enable us to hear our inner voices, to comprehend reality with both our hearts and our minds, puts us in touch with divine essence. Practicing the art of loving is one way we sustain contact with our "higher self." In Linell Cady's essay "A Feminist Christian Vision," she suggests that the divine is not a being but rather the *unifying of being:*

> The divine spirit of love motivates and empowers humans to see more clearly and to act more justly by identifying the self with that which lies beyond its narrow borders. Notice the correlation between the self and the divine in this theological vision. From this perspective the self is not a substantial entity, complete and defined, but a reality always in the process of being created through the dynamic of love, which continually alters its boundaries and identity. Similarly, the divine is not perfected and completed being but processes that seek to expand and perfect being.

In Zora Neale Hurston's novel *Their Eyes Were Watching God,* Janie is able to experience her divine essence first through union with nature and then through the experience of erotic love. Yet, she ultimately fashions a life in the spirit that is fundamentally rooted in her understanding of the value of human life and intersubjective communion where she experiences the unity of all life.

Taking time to experience ourselves in solitude is one way that we can regain a sense of the divine that can feel the spirit moving in our lives. Solitude is essential to the spiritual for it is there that we cannot only commune with divine spirits but also listen to our inner voice. One way to transform the lonely feeling that overwhelms some of us is to enter that lonely place and find there a stillness that enables us to hear the soul speak. Henri Nouwen, in *Out of Solitude,* reminds us to attend to our need for solitude: "Somewhere we know that without a lonely place our lives are in danger. Somewhere we know that without silence words lose their meaning, that without listening speaking no longer heals. Somewhere we know that without a lonely place our actions quickly become empty gestures."

Black women have not focused sufficiently on our need for contemplative spaces. We are often "too busy" to find time for solitude. And yet it is in the stillness that we also learn how to be with ourselves in a spirit of acceptance and peace. Then when we re-enter community, we are able to extend this acceptance to others. Without knowing how to be alone, we cannot know how to be with others and sustain the necessary autonomy. Yet, many of us live in fear of being alone. To meditate, to go into solitude and silence, we find a way to be empowered by aloneness. It is helpful to have days of silence, times that allow us to practice what Thich Nhat Hanh calls "the miracle of mindfulness." He uses the term mindfulness to "refer to keeping one's consciousness alive to the present reality." Worry and stress often keep us fixated on the future, so that we lose sight of the present, of what it means to be here and now. Mindfulness helps us find a way back to the present. Black women's lives are enriched when we are able to be fully aware, to be mindful. Meditation enhances our capacity to practice mindfulness and should not be dismissed.

Black women who are more engaged with conventional religious life may find it helpful to engage both in silent and spoken prayer. In his essay "Pray for Your Own Discovery," Thomas Merton suggests that we "seek God perfectly" when we "entertain silence" in our hearts and "listen for the voice of God." Prayer allows the individual to speak directly with God, with spirits and angels. In the act of prayer, individual black women who may have tremendous difficulty baring their soul can find a space to speak, to pour out their hearts' longing and, in the act of praying, gain a sense of direction. Prayers often guide, leading us into fuller awareness of who we are and what we are meant to do.

Dreams can also serve as guides to the spirits. Black women have had long traditions of dream interpretation, passing these skills from generation to generation. I grew up in a world of black women who were serious about the interpretation of dreams, who knew that dreams not only tell us what we need to know about the self but guide us when we are lost. Yet when I went to college, I abandoned the practice of giving close attention to my dream life. I have returned to that practice, recognizing it to be a space of empowerment. When we are in need of greater self-understanding or guidance, it can be helpful to keep a dream book, a notebook where we write down our dreams and our reflections and thoughts about them.

Living a life in the spirit, whatever our practices, can help black women sustain ourselves as we chart new life journeys. Many of us have lifeways very different from those any other generation of black women have known. Madonna Kolbenschlag suggests in *Lost in the Land of Oz* that all women today will know seasons of loneliness unlike those experienced by previous generations: "Women, more so than men, are trying out a new myth. They have no role models or generational anchors to lean on in trying out a new story, and so it is scary and lonely...The orphaned woman has broken with many of the old codes of normality, but has not yet found what will take its place." Nurturing our spiritual selves we can find within the courage to sustain new journeys and the will to invent new ways to live and view the world. In *The Feminist Mystic,* Mary Giles invites us to celebrate this positionality, where we are poised between the old and the new, and urges us to be guided by a dynamic love:

> To live and to love and to create are one. In living, loving, and creating we move in mystery, alert to possibility, bereft of models from the past and without hint of one to come. In the absence of models we experience absolute freedom, and in freedom, risk, responsibility and the joy of being opened to whatever the moment may bring forth in us.

Certainly black women seeking self-recovery are charting new journeys. Although I have read countless self-help books, the vast majority do not even acknowledge the existence of black people. It is a new journey for black women to begin to write and talk more openly about aspects of our reality that are not talked about.

At times I found writing about some of the issues in this book very saddening. And I would say to Tanya, my play daughter and comrade, that I felt writing this book would "break my heart." We talked often about why individuals who suffer intensely often cannot find ways to give their anguish words. To speak about certain pains is also to remember them. And in the act of remembering we are called to relive, to know again much that we would suppress and forget. This book hardly speaks to all that needs to be said. And yet so much of it was hard to say. And sisters have asked me: "Aren't you afraid that black people will punish you for saying things about black experience they feel should not be said?" I gain courage from my spiritual life, from the sense that I am called in writing to give testimony, that it is my spiritual vocation. I call to mind the biblical passage from "Romans" that says: "Do not be conformed to this world but be ye transformed by the renewing of your mind, that you may know what the will of God is." Reading inspirational writing is an essential part of self-recovery. We are sustained by one another's testimony when we find ourselves faltering or falling into despair.

Although, I had been thinking for years that I would write this book, it never came. Thoughts, ideas, and memories were inside me but they did not manifest themselves in words. Suddenly, in the past months, black women were asking me where they could find the Sisters of the Yam book. And there would be such disappointment when I would say that it had not yet been written. Again it was the sense of urgency I felt from sister comrades that made me think "now is the time." Yet as the writing progressed, I began to feel depressed and frustrated that other plans had fallen through. One evening as I sat in stillness, I heard an inner voice telling me that I was meant to be here in my house doing this book right now. And I felt peaceful and calm. This to me is a manifestation of the power that comes from living a life in the spirit. In his essay "Healing the Heart of Justice," Victor Lewis shares the insight that it is a necessity for us to move against fear and despair to embrace healing visions:

> To value ourselves rightly, infinitely, released from shame and self-rejection, implies knowing that we are claimed by the totality of life. To share in a loving community and vision that magnifies our strength and banishes fear and despair, here, we find the solid ground from which justice can flow like a mighty stream. Here, we find the fire that burns away the confusion that oppression heaped upon us during our childhood weakness. Here, we can see what needs to be done and find the strength to do it. To value ourselves rightly. To love one another. This is to heal the heart of justice.

The purpose of this writing was to add to that growing body of literature that hopes to enable us to value ourselves, rightly, fully.

In spiritual solidarity, black women have the potential to be a community of faith that acts collectively to transform our world. When we heal the woundedness inside us, when we attend to the inner love-seeking, love-starved child, we make ourselves ready to enter more fully into community. We can experience the totality of life because we have become fully life-affirming. Like our ancestors using our powers to the fullest, we share the secrets of healing and come to know sustained joy.

# Bibliography

Ali, Shahrazad. *The Blackman's Guide to Understanding the Blackwo-man*, Philadelphia: Civilized Publications, 1989.

Anand, Margo. *The Art of Sexual Ecstasy*, Los Angeles: Jeremy Tarcher, 1989.

Angelou, Maya. *I Know Why the Caged Bird Sings*, New York: Bantam, 1970.

Bambara, Toni Cade, ed. *The Black Woman*, New York: New American Library, 1970.

Bambara, Toni Cade. *The Salt Eaters*, New York: Random House, 1981.

Benjamin, Jessica. *Bonds of Love: Psychoanalysis, Feminism and the Problem of Domination*, New York: Pantheon, 1988.

Berrigan, Daniel and Thich Nhat Hanh. *The Raft Is Not The Shore*, Boston: Beacon Press, 1975.

Berry, Wendell. *The Unsettling of America: Culture and Agriculture*, New York: Avon, 1977.

Beverly, Victoria. *Hard Times Cotton Mill Girls*, Ithaca, NY: ILR Press, 1986.

Clark, Septima Poinsette. *Ready from Within: Septima Clark and the Civil Rights Movement*, Navarro, CA: Wild Trees Press, 1986.

Cleage, Pearl. *Mad At Miles*, Southfield, MI: Cleage Group, 1990.

Chisolm, Shirley. *Unbought and Unbossed*, New York: Avon, 1970.

Cooley, Paula, *et al.*, eds. *Embodied Love: Sensuality and Relationship as Feminist Values*, San Fransisco: Harper and Row, 1987.

Cowan, Lynn. *Masochism: A Jungian View*, Dallas, TX: Spring Publications, 1982.

Dunbar, Paul Laurence. *The Complete Poems of Paul Laurence Dunbar*, New York: Dodd, Mead & Co., 1980.

Fox, Arnold and Barry. *Wake up! You're Alive,* Deerfield Beach, FL: Health Communications, 1988.

Fox, Matthew. "Honoring Howard Thurnon," Oakland, ÇA: *Creation,* Volume VIII, Number 2, March-April 1991.

Fry, Gladys Marie. *Stitched from the Soul: Slave Quilts from the Ante-Bellum South,* New York: Dutton, 1990.

Giles, Mary, ed. *The Feminist Mystic,* New York: Crossroad, 1982.

Grudin, Eva. *Stitching Memories: African-American Story Quilts,* Williamstown, MA: William College Museum of Art, 1990.

Hansberry, Lorraine. *To Be Young, Gifted, and Black,* New York: New American Library, 1969.

Hay, Louise. *The AIDS Book,* Carson, CA: Hay House, 1988.

Hay, Louise. *You Can Heal Your Life,* Carson, CA: Hay House, 1987.

hooks, bell. *Talking Back,* Boston: South End Press, 1989.

Hurston, Zora Neale. *Their Eyes Were Watching God,* Chicago: University of Illinois Press, 1991.

Jacobs, Harriet A. *Incidents in the Life of a Slave Girl: Written by Herself,* Cambridge, MA: Harvard University Press, 1987.

Jeffers, Susan. *Feel the Fear and Do It Anyway,* New York: Fawcett Columbine, 1987.

Jones-Jackson, Patricia. *When Roots Die,* Athens, GA: University of Georgia Press, 1987.

Keen, Sam. *Apology For Wonder,* New York: Harper and Row, 1969.

Keen, Sam. *The Passionate Life: Stages of Learning,* New York: Harper and Row, 1983.

King, Martin Luther, Jr. *A Testament of Hope,* edited by James Melvin Washington, New York: Harper & Row, 1986.

Kolbenschlag, Madonna. *Lost in the Land of Oz,* New York: Harper and Row, 1989.

Kubler-Ross, Elizabeth, ed. *Death: The Final Stage of Growth,* New York: Simon and Schuster, 1975.

Kubler-Ross, Elizabeth. *On Death and Dying,* New York: Macmillan, 1969.

Lane, Lunsford. "The Narrative of Lunsford Lane," *Five Slave Narratives,* edited by William L. Katz, New York: Arno Press, 1968.

Lerner, Harriet Goldhor. *The Dance of Anger,* New York: Harper and Row, 1985.

Lerner, Harriet Goldhor. *The Dance of Intimacy,* New York: Harper and Row, 1989.

Logan, Onnie Lee, as told to Katherine Clark. *Motherwit,* New York: Dutton, 1989.

Lorde, Audre. *The Black Unicorn,* New York: W.W. Norton, 1978.

Lorde, Audre. *The Cancer Journals,* Oakland, CA: Aunt Lute, 1980.

Lorde, Audre. *Sister Outsider,* Freedom, CA: Crossing Press, 1984.

Lorde, Audre. *Zami,* Freedom, CA: Crossing Press, 1982.

Madhubuti, Haki, ed. *Confusion by any Other Name,* Chicago: Third World Press, 1990.

Marshall, Paule. *Praisesong for the Widow,* New York: G. P. Putnam's Sons, 1983.

McClain, Leanita. *A Foot in Each World: Articles and Essays,* Evanston, IL: Northwestern University Press, 1986.

Merton, Thomas. *Love and Living,* New York: Harcourt, Brace, Jovanovich, 1979.

Merton, Thomas. *New Seeds of Contemplation,* New York: New Directions, 1961.

Moody, Anne. *Coming of Age in Mississippi,* New York: Dell Publishing, 1968.

Morrison, Toni. *Beloved,* New York: Alfred Knopf, 1987.

Morrison, Toni. *The Bluest Eye,* New York: Pocket Books, 1970.

Morrison, Toni. *Song of Solomon,* New York: New American Library, 1977.

Morrison, Toni. *Sula,* New York: New American Library, 1973.

Nhat Hanh, Thich. *Interbeing,* Berkeley, CA: Parallex Press, 1987.

Nhat Hanh, Thich. *Peace Is Every Step,* New York: Bantam, 1991.

Nhat Hanh, Thich. *The Heart of Understanding,* Berkeley, CA: Parallex Press, 1988.

Nhat Hanh, Thich. *The Miracle of Mindfulness,* Boston: Beacon Press, 1975.

Nouwen, Henri. *Out of Solitude,* Indiana: Ave Maria Press, 1974.

# SISTERS OF THE YAM

Peck, M. Scott. *The Road Less Traveled*, New York: Simon & Schuster, 1978.

Peele, Stanton. *Diseasing of America: Addiction Treatment Out of Control*, New York: Houghton Mifflin, 1991.

Peele, Stanton. *Love and Addiction*, New York: New American Library, 1975.

Scott, Kesho Yvonne. *The Habit of Surviving: Black Women's Strategies for Life*, New Brunswick, NJ: Rutgers University Press, 1991.

Shaef, Anne Wilson. *When Society Becomes an Addict*, New York: Harper and Row, 1987.

Shange, Ntozake. *Riding the Moon in Texas*, New York: St. Martin's Press, 1987.

Shange, Ntozake. *Sassafras, Cypress and Indigo*, New York: St. Martin's Press, 1982.

Shange, Ntozake. *The Love Space Demand: A Continuing Saga*, New York: St. Martin's Press, 1992.

Siegel, Bernie. *Love, Medicine and Miracles*, New York: Harper and Row, 1986.

Siegel, Bernie. *Peace, Love and Healing*, New York: Harper and Row, 1989.

Sinetar, Marsha. *Do What You Love, The Money Will Follow*, New York: Paulist Press, 1987.

Teish, Luisah. *Jambalaya*, New York: Harper and Row, 1985.

Trungpa, Chogyam. *Shambhala*, Boston: Shambhala Publications, 1984.

Walker, Alice. *In Search of Our Mother's Gardens*, New York: Harvest/HBJ, 1983.

Walker, Alice. *Living by the Word*, New York: Harcourt Brace Jovanivich, 1988.

Walker, Alice. *The Color Purple*, New York: Harcourt Brace Jovanivich, 1982.

Walker, Alice. *The Temple of My Familiar*, New York: Harcourt Brace Jovanivich, 1989.

White, Evelyn. *The Black Women's Health Book: Speaking for Ourselves*, Seattle, WA: Seal Press, 1990.

194

# About bell hooks

Born and raised in a rural community in Kentucky, bell hooks has become a renowned teacher, author, and speaker on the issues of personal empowerment and the politics of race, gender, and class. Besides having taught English, African American Studies, and Women's Studies at Oberlin College, Yale University, and City College of New York, hooks has published seven critically-acclaimed books with South End Press.

Her first book, *Ain't I A Woman,* published in 1981, was named one of the "twenty most influential women's books of the last twenty years" in a *Publishers Weekly* poll in May 1992. *Publishers Weekly* also named her recent book, *Breaking Bread,* co-authored with Cornel West, "one of the twenty-five best books of 1992." The *Village Voice Literary Supplement* argued that her book, *Black Looks: Race and Representation,* was "one of the twenty-five best books of 1992." In 1991, hooks received the Before Columbus Foundation's American Book Award for *Yearning: Race, Gender, and Cultural Politics.* In 1990, the American Studies Association Critic's Choice Panel chose *Talking Back: Thinking Feminist, Thinking Black* as one of the most outstanding recent books in the area of Educational Studies.

Her essays have appeared in numerous journals and magazines, including *Ms., Tricycle, On the Issues, The Other Side, Essence,* and *Emerge.* Her bi-monthly column "Sisters of the Yam" has been a regular feature in *Z Magazine* for the last five years. She is also much in demand as a speaker at conferences and campuses across the country and around the world.

# About South End Press

South End Press is a nonprofit, collectively run book publisher with over 175 titles in print. Since our founding in 1977, we have tried to meet the needs of readers who are exploring, or are already committed to, the politics of radical social change.

Our goal is to publish books that encourage critical thinking and constructive action on the key political, cultural, social, economic, and ecological issues shaping life in the United States and in the world today. In this way, we hope to give expression to a wide diversity of democratic social movements and to provide an alternative to the products of corporate publishing.

If you would like a free catalog of South End Press books or information about our membership program—which offers two free books and a 40% discount on all titles—please write us at South End Press, 116 Saint Botolph Street, Boston, MA 02115.

# Other titles by bell hooks

**Black Looks:**
**Race and Representation**

**Breaking Bread:**
**Insurgent Black Intellectual Life**
(with Cornel West)

**Yearning:**
**Race, Gender, and Cultural Politics**

**Talking Back:**
**Thinking Feminist, Thinking Black**

**Feminist Theory:**
**From Margin to Center**

**Ain't I a Woman:**
**Black Women and Feminism**